# Southern Living®
## ALL-TIME FAVORITE
# LIGHT
## MEALS

# Southern Living®
## ALL-TIME FAVORITE
# LIGHT
# MEALS

Compiled and Edited by
Jean Wickstrom Liles

Oxmoor
House®

Copyright 1997 by Oxmoor House, Inc.
Book Division of Southern Progress Corporation
P.O. Box 2463, Birmingham, Alabama 35201

Library of Congress Catalog Number: 96-68033
ISBN: 0-8487-2229-9
Manufactured in the United States of America
First Printing 1997

Editor-in-Chief: Nancy Fitzpatrick Wyatt
Editorial Director, Special Interest Publications: Ann H. Harvey
Senior Foods Editor: Susan Carlisle Payne
Senior Editor, Editorial Services: Olivia Kindig Wells
Art Director: James Boone

## Southern Living® ALL-TIME FAVORITE LIGHT MEALS

Menu and Recipe Consultant: Jean Wickstrom Liles
Assistant Editor: Kelly Hooper Troiano
Associate Foods Editor: Anne Chappell Cain, M.S., M.P.H., R.D.
Copy Editor: Jane Phares
Editorial Assistants: Valorie J. Cooper, Catherine S. Ritter
Indexer: Mary Ann Laurens
Concept Designer: Melissa Jones Clark
Designer: Rita Yerby
Senior Photographers: Jim Bathie; Charles Walton IV, *Southern Living* magazine
Photographers: Ralph Anderson; Tina Cornett, J. Savage Gibson, Sylvia Martin, *Southern Living* magazine
Senior Photo Stylists: Kay E. Clarke; Leslie Byars Simpson, *Southern Living* magazine
Photo Stylist: Virginia R. Cravens
Production and Distribution Director: Phillip Lee
Associate Production Manager: Vanessa Cobbs Richardson
Production Assistant: Valerie L. Heard

Our appreciation to the editorial staff of *Southern Living* magazine and to the Southern Progress Corporation
library staff for their contributions to this volume.

Cover: Grilled Flank Steak with Sweet Peppers (complete menu on page 50)
Page 1: Grilled Tuna with Poblano Salsa (complete menu on page 93)
Page 2: Roast Turkey Breast and Gravy (complete menu on page 116)

### We're Here for You!

We at Oxmoor House are
dedicated to serving you with
reliable information that expands
your imagination and enriches
your life. We welcome your
comments and suggestions. Please
write us at:

Oxmoor House, Inc.
Editor, *All-Time Favorite*
*Light Meals*
2100 Lakeshore Drive
Birmingham, AL 35209

# Contents

# Keep It Light!

Fret no more about planning flavorful, low-calorie, low-fat meals. With this cookbook you have over 45 menus to choose from for weeknights, special occasions, and holidays. And even more important, each of these taste-tempting meals fits into a healthy, low-fat lifestyle.

## Nutritional Analysis

All menus in *All-Time Favorite Light Meals* meet the guidelines for healthy eating. The total calories for each menu come from these sources:

- at least 50 percent from carbohydrates
- about 20 percent from protein
- less than 30 percent from fat

Each recipe has been kitchen-tested by a staff of home economists, and registered dietitians have determined the nutritional information using a computer system that analyzes each ingredient.

The nutrient grid following each recipe includes calories per serving and the percentage of calories from fat. Also, the grid lists the grams of total fat, saturated fat, protein, and carbohydrate, and the milligrams of cholesterol and sodium per serving. The nutrient values are as accurate as possible and are based on these assumptions:

- All meats are trimmed of fat and skin before cooking.
- When the recipe calls for cooked pasta, rice, or noodles, the analysis is based on cooking without additional salt or fat.
- Fruits and vegetables included in the ingredient list are not peeled unless specified.
- When fresh fruits or vegetables are included as accompaniments to a recipe, the menu analysis reflects about ½ cup serving of these in the menu calculation.
- When a range is given for an ingredient, the lesser amount is calculated.
- A percentage of alcohol calories evaporates when heated; this reduction is reflected in the calculations.
- When a marinade is used, only the amount of marinade absorbed is calculated.
- Garnishes and optional ingredients are not calculated.

## Meal Planning

Preparing meals that look and taste good with seemingly little effort takes advance planning and organizing. This involves creating menus, taking stock of the pantry and refrigerator, and making grocery lists. These tips should help make your menu planning and preparation easier.

• Keep meals simple. A main course, salad, and dessert make a well-rounded meal.

• Plan weekly menus to include your family's favorite recipes as well as new ones you want to try.

• Take an inventory of your pantry, refrigerator, and freezer, and then plan meals around what you have on hand, including leftovers. Fill in the "holes" with new recipes.

Take inventory of your pantry.

• Write out your grocery list as you plan menus to be sure that you have all the ingredients on hand.

• Double a recipe or make two batches to suit your needs. If a recipe yields more than needed, freeze or refrigerate the food to serve another day.

Freeze foods prepared in advance.

• Take advantage of "planned leftovers" or include recipes in your menu that will leave leftovers you can use later.

• Plan recipes that can be prepared in advance. Cook foods that take hours to bake or simmer on the weekend, or prepare a recipe in the evening to add to your meal the next night.

• Plan ahead for company or holiday dinners. Make your shopping list and plan your schedule in advance.

• Always check a product's expiration date to be sure you're buying the freshest package.

• Keep a notepad and pencil in your kitchen to jot down ingredients that need replenishing.

## Lighten Your Recipes

As you become familiar with techniques and ingredients for lighter cooking, preparing nutritious recipes will become second nature.

When you cook, try steaming, sautéing, broiling, boiling, grilling, or stir-frying your food choices instead of deep-fat or pan-frying them. Avoid boiling foods in large amounts of water because this depletes water-soluble nutrients in the foods. Prevent meat from cooking in excess fat when roasting by placing it on a rack in a roasting pan.

Observing these cooking techniques will give you a good start toward preparing foods that are lower in fat and calories. And by steaming or cooking vegetables in just a little water, you'll retain the water-soluble vitamins such as vitamin C.

Steam vegetables to retain nutrients.

Cooking methods alone, however, will not make a recipe low in fat or cholesterol. By making smart low-fat substitutions in the ingredients, you can make a recipe more nutritious without decreasing the flavor of the food.

Refer to the chart on page 8 for suggestions on how to lighten some of your own favorite recipes.

## Simple Ways To Lighten Recipes

In lightening recipes included in this cookbook, the primary goal was to reduce fat, cholesterol, and calories. The tips below will help you to do the same thing when you are making changes in your own favorite dishes. Not all substitutions work for all recipes, so you may need to do some experimenting.

| Instead of . . . | Try . . . | Save . . . Fat (g) | Chol (mg) | Cal |
|---|---|---|---|---|
| Baking chocolate (1 ounce) | 3 tablespoons dry cocoa plus 2 teaspoons sugar and 1 tablespoon water | 13 | 0 | 70 |
| Butter, margarine, shortening, or vegetable oil (1 tablespoon) | ½ the amount called for in recipe; or 1 tablespoon reduced-calorie margarine; or an equal amount of unsweetened applesauce (in baked goods only) | 6 6 95 | 15 31 12 | 51 52 31 |
| Cheese (1 ounce) | ½ the amount called for in recipe; or 1 ounce reduced-fat or part-skim (with 5 or fewer grams of fat per ounce) | 5 4 | 15 12 | 57 30 |
| Chicken broth, canned, regular (1 cup) | 1 cup reduced-sodium, fat-free, canned chicken broth | 4 | 0 | 19 |
| Cream or half-and-half (1 tablespoon) | 1 tablespoon evaporated skimmed milk | 3 | 9 | 17 |
| Cream of mushroom soup (10¾-ounce can) | 10¾-ounce can 99% fat-free cream of mushroom soup | 18 | 0 | 151 |
| Egg (1 large) | ¼ cup egg substitute or 2 large egg whites | 6 6 | 258 258 | 61 59 |
| Ground beef (1 ounce) | 1 ounce 93% or 96% low-fat ground beef; or 1 ounce lean ground turkey | 3 4 | 4 4 | 23 |
| Mayonnaise (1 tablespoon) | 1 tablespoon reduced-calorie mayonnaise; or fat-free mayonnaise; or 1½ teaspoons reduced-calorie mayonnaise mixed with 1½ teaspoons plain nonfat yogurt | 6 11 9 | 2 8 5 | 55 86 73 |
| Pecans, chopped (½ cup) | ¼ cup toasted (this works with any type nut) | 20 | 0 | 199 |
| Sour cream (½ cup) | ½ cup plain nonfat yogurt; or ½ cup nonfat sour cream (for baked goods, add 1½ teaspoons flour to each cup of yogurt or nonfat sour cream) | 24 24 | 49 51 | 182 166 |
| Whole milk (1 cup) | 1 cup skim milk | 8 | 29 | 63 |

## Sizing Up a Serving

To serve a balanced, nutritious diet, you have to know how much of each food to serve. The serving sizes listed in the chart below are guidelines, but also keep in mind these suggestions:

• Count your serving size as more than one serving if you eat a significantly larger portion than the suggested serving size.

• Use the same serving size for children age six or older as you would for an adult.

• Count two-thirds of the adult serving size as one serving for children ages two to five.

• Ask your physician or a registered dietitian for advice on feeding children under age two. Fat should not be restricted in their diets.

## What Is a Serving?

Under the FDA regulations, nutrition labels are standardized. Serving size is based on the portion customarily consumed by an average person over the age of four years. The list of portions below count as one serving.

**Breads, Cereals, Rice, and Pasta**
1 slice bread
½ bagel
1 English muffin
1 hamburger or hotdog bun
1 ounce ready-to-eat-cereal
½ cup cooked cereal
½ cup cooked pasta
½ cup cooked rice

**Fruits**
½ cup chopped fresh fruit
½ cup canned fruit
½ cup cooked fruit
1 medium-size piece fresh fruit
¾ cup fruit juice

**Vegetables**
1 cup raw leafy vegetables
½ cup chopped raw vegetables
½ cup cooked vegetables
¾ cup vegetable juice

**Milk, Yogurt, and Cheese**
1 cup skim milk
1 cup nonfat or low-fat yogurt
1½ ounces reduced-fat cheese
2 ounces reduced-fat process cheese

**Meats, Poultry, Fish, Dried Beans, Eggs, and Nuts**
2 to 3 ounces cooked lean meat, poultry, or fish
½ cup cooked dried beans
1 egg
¼ cup egg substitute
2 tablespoons peanut butter

# Staple Ingredients Checklist

Here's how to keep your kitchen stocked for cooking healthy in a hurry.

## In the Pantry:

These ingredients will keep six months to one year.

### Baking Supplies

Baking and biscuit mix, fat-free
Baking powder
Baking soda
Chocolate, semisweet mini-morsels
Cocoa, unsweetened
Cornstarch
Flours: all-purpose
  cake
  whole wheat
Milk: nonfat dry milk powder
  canned evaporated skimmed milk
Oats, quick-cooking
Oils: olive
  vegetable
Sugar: granulated
  light brown
  powdered
Sweeteners: honey
  light-colored corn syrup
Vegetable cooking spray: plain
  butter-flavored
  olive oil-flavored

### Fruits and Vegetables

Dried fruit: apples
  apricots
  prunes
  raisins
Fruits, canned, in light syrup or in
  juice: unsweetened applesauce
  apricot halves
  whole berry cranberry sauce
  mandarin oranges
  sliced peaches
  pear halves
  crushed pineapple
Juices, unsweetened: apple
  grape
Tomato products, no-salt-added:
  juice
  low-fat pasta sauce
  paste
  sauce
  whole tomatoes
Tomatoes, sun-dried
Vegetables, canned: green chiles
  ripe olives
  pimientos
  pumpkin
  roasted red pepper in water
  water chestnuts

### Grains, Legumes, and Pasta

Beans, canned, no-salt-added if
  available: black
  black-eyed peas
  garbanzos (chick peas)
  kidney
  navy
  pinto
  red
Bulgur wheat
Couscous
Lentils, dried
Pasta, dry: egg noodles
  elbow macaroni
  fettuccine (plain or spinach)
  spaghetti
Rice: instant white and brown
  long-grain white and brown

### Condiments and Seasonings

Italian dressing, oil-free
Jams, no-sugar-added: apple jelly
  orange marmalade
  raspberry spread
Mayonnaise, light or nonfat
Mustards: Dijon
  honey
  prepared
Seasoning sauces: hot sauce
  reduced-calorie ketchup
  no-salt-added salsa
  low-sodium soy sauce
  low-sodium Worcestershire sauce
Vinegars: balsamic
  cider
  white

### Miscellaneous

Bouillon granules: beef-flavored
  chicken-flavored
Broth, canned: low-sodium beef
  low-sodium chicken
  vegetable
Crackers, fat-free
Garlic-in-a-jar
Gelatin, unflavored
Graham crackers
Peanut butter, reduced-fat
Tuna, canned in water

## In the Refrigerator:

These items will keep at least a week, but check freshness dates before purchasing.

Nonfat buttermilk
Cheeses: reduced-fat Cheddar or
  other semifirm cheeses
  light process cream cheese
  grated Parmesan cheese
  light ricotta cheese
Eggs
Stick margarine
Seasonings, for convenience:
  fresh jalapeño chiles
  gingerroot, cut into ½-inch pieces
Nonfat sour cream
Plain nonfat yogurt

## In the Freezer:

These items can be frozen two months to one year if kept at 0 degrees or colder.

Breads: corn and flour tortillas
  French loaves
  hamburger buns
Chicken, skinned and boned breast
  halves
Frozen egg substitute
Fruits, unsweetened: blueberries
  peaches
  raspberries
  strawberries
Juice concentrates: grape
  lemonade
  orange
Phyllo pastry
Frozen cooked salad shrimp
Vegetables: asparagus
  green beans
  lima beans
  broccoli
  carrots
  whole kernel corn
  chopped onion
  English peas
  snow pea pods
  chopped pepper
  spinach
Frozen nonfat yogurt

# What's for Dinner?

Weeknight dinners don't have to be dull. With these quick-fix menus you can serve festive family pleasers any evening with very little effort.

**Stuffed Flank Steak with Noodles, Snow Peas and Red Pepper**

Green Beans and Potatoes, New-Fashioned Apple Cobbler, Oven-Fried Catfish

Hungarian Goulash, Honey-Glazed Carrots, Fruited Cheese Pie, Veal Marsala

**Hearts of Romaine with Caper Vinaigrette, New Potato Medley**

Bean and Cornbread Casserole (complete menu on page 32)

# Fit for Company

---

## Stuffed Flank Steak with Noodles

1 cup chopped fresh spinach
1 cup sliced green onions
⅓ cup freshly grated Parmesan cheese
½ cup frozen artichoke hearts, thawed, drained, and chopped
¼ cup soft breadcrumbs
½ teaspoon freshly ground pepper
¼ teaspoon salt
1½ pounds cubed flank steak
2 cloves garlic, crushed
2 tablespoons low-sodium Worcestershire sauce
Vegetable cooking spray
¼ pound fresh mushrooms, sliced
1 small onion, thinly sliced
1 teaspoon chicken-flavored bouillon granules
½ cup water
2 sprigs fresh parsley
1 bay leaf
3 cups cooked fettuccine (cooked without salt or fat)
1 tablespoon cornstarch
2 tablespoons water

**Combine** first 5 ingredients; set aside.

**Sprinkle** pepper and salt over flank steak; spread spinach mixture in center of meat within 1 inch of sides. Roll up jellyroll fashion, starting with long side. Secure at 2-inch intervals with string.

**Rub** crushed garlic over steak roll, and drizzle with Worcestershire sauce.

**Coat** a nonstick skillet with cooking spray; place over medium-high heat until hot. Brown steak roll on all sides; transfer to a 13- x 9- x 2-inch pan. Combine mushrooms and onion; place around steak.

**Dissolve** bouillon granules in ½ cup water; add to pan. Add parsley and bay leaf.

**Cover** and bake at 300° for 50 minutes or until meat is tender.

**Transfer** steak to a serving platter. Let stand 15 minutes; remove string and slice steak. Arrange cooked fettuccine around steak slices on platter. Keep warm.

**Place** pan drippings, mushrooms, and onion in a medium saucepan. Remove and discard parsley and bay leaf.

**Combine** cornstarch and 2 tablespoons water; stir into pan drippings. Bring mixture to a boil; boil 1 minute, stirring constantly. Serve gravy over steak. **Yield: 6 servings.**

**Note:** To cube flank steak, ask butcher to run steak through meat tenderizer twice.

PER SERVING: 350 CALORIES (34% FROM FAT)
FAT 13.2G (SATURATED FAT 5.8G)
PROTEIN 29.8G CARBOHYDRATE 27.3G
CHOLESTEROL 61MG SODIUM 471MG

## Snow Peas and Red Pepper

Olive oil-flavored vegetable cooking spray
3 cups snow pea pods, trimmed
1 cup diced sweet red pepper
1 small clove garlic, minced
2 teaspoons sesame seeds
½ teaspoon salt-free lemon-pepper seasoning
¼ teaspoon Chinese 5-spice powder

**Coat** a large, nonstick skillet with cooking spray; place over medium-high heat until hot. Add snow peas and sweet red pepper; cook 5 minutes, stirring constantly.

**Add** garlic, sesame seeds, and seasonings; cook 2 to 3 minutes or until vegetables are crisp-tender, stirring constantly. **Yield: 6 (½-cup) servings.**

PER SERVING: 48 CALORIES (17% FROM FAT)
FAT 0.9G (SATURATED FAT 0.1G)
PROTEIN 3.0G CARBOHYDRATE 7.5G
CHOLESTEROL 0MG SODIUM 4MG

# Lemon Curd with Berries

½ cup sugar
¼ cup cornstarch
¼ teaspoon salt
2 cups skim milk
¼ cup frozen egg substitute, thawed
1½ teaspoons grated lemon rind
¼ cup lemon juice
1½ cups fresh or frozen raspberries, thawed
1½ cups fresh or frozen blueberries, thawed
Garnish: fresh mint sprigs

**Combine** first 3 ingredients in a heavy saucepan; gradually add milk, stirring well. Cook over medium heat, stirring constantly, until mixture thickens.

**Remove** from heat; gradually add egg substitute to hot mixture, stirring constantly with a wire whisk. Cook over medium-low heat 2 minutes; remove from heat, and cool slightly. Stir in lemon rind and juice; cool.

**Alternate** layers of berries and lemon curd into 6 parfait glasses. Chill until ready to serve. Garnish, if desired. **Yield: 6 servings.**

PER SERVING: 156 CALORIES (2% FROM FAT)
FAT 0.4G (SATURATED FAT 0.1G)
PROTEIN 4.4G CARBOHYDRATE 35.3G
CHOLESTEROL 2MG SODIUM 158MG

Lemon Curd with Berries

## Before You Squeeze

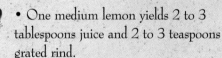

• One medium lemon yields 2 to 3 tablespoons juice and 2 to 3 teaspoons grated rind.

• To remove the most lemon juice from an unpeeled fruit, use one of these methods: roll lemon firmly on a countertop; microwave at HIGH 20 seconds; or submerge in hot water 15 minutes.

• If the recipe calls for grated rind, remember to grate lemon before squeezing it.

Hungarian Goulash and Honey-Glazed Carrots

# An Autumn Favorite

### Serves 4

Hungarian Goulash
Honey-Glazed Carrots
Tossed green salad (1½ cups salad and 1 tablespoon fat-free dressing per serving)
Fruited Cheese Pie (1 slice per serving)

*Total Calories per Serving: 618*
*(Calories from Fat: 21%)*

# Hungarian Goulash

1  pound lean, boneless top round steak
2  teaspoons vegetable oil
1¼  cups coarsely chopped onion
1  cup green pepper strips
2½  cups chopped fresh tomato
1¼  to 1½ cups water
1  tablespoon paprika
½  teaspoon salt
¼  teaspoon pepper
2  cups hot cooked brown rice (cooked without salt or fat)

**Trim** all visible fat from steak; cut steak into bite-size pieces. Cook in hot oil in a large skillet over medium heat until browned, stirring often.

**Add** onion and green pepper; cook 5 minutes, stirring often. Stir in tomato and next 4 ingredients.

**Bring** to a boil; cover, reduce heat, and simmer 45 minutes or until tender, adding additional water, if necessary. Serve over rice. **Yield: 4 servings.**

PER SERVING: 341 CALORIES (22% FROM FAT)
FAT 8.5G (SATURATED FAT 2.4G)
PROTEIN 30.5G CARBOHYDRATE 35.6G
CHOLESTEROL 65MG SODIUM 370MG

# Honey-Glazed Carrots

4½  cups sliced carrot (about 2 pounds)
1  tablespoon reduced-calorie margarine
1½  tablespoons honey
1  tablespoon lemon juice

**Arrange** carrot in a steamer basket over boiling water. Cover and steam 4 to 8 minutes.

**Melt** margarine in a skillet over medium heat; add honey and lemon juice, stirring well. Add warm carrot; toss. **Yield: 4 (1-cup) servings.**

PER SERVING: 93 CALORIES (19% FROM FAT)
FAT 2.0G (SATURATED FAT 0.3G)
PROTEIN 1.3G CARBOHYDRATE 19.4G
CHOLESTEROL 0MG SODIUM 71MG

# Fruited Cheese Pie

1  cup graham cracker crumbs
3  tablespoons reduced-calorie margarine, melted
2  tablespoons sugar
Butter-flavored cooking spray
1  envelope unflavored gelatin
¼  cup cold water
1  cup nonfat cottage cheese
½  cup plain nonfat yogurt
¼  cup sugar
½  cup unsweetened pineapple juice
1  teaspoon lemon juice
⅛  teaspoon ground cinnamon
1  (11-ounce) can mandarin orange sections in light syrup, drained
2  tablespoons low-sugar orange marmalade, melted

**Combine** first 3 ingredients in a small bowl; firmly press crumb mixture over bottom and up sides of a 9-inch pieplate.

**Coat** crust with cooking spray; bake at 350° for 7 to 9 minutes. Cool on a wire rack.

**Sprinkle** gelatin over water in a small saucepan; let stand 1 minute. Cook over low heat, stirring until gelatin dissolves (about 2 minutes).

**Combine** cottage cheese and next 5 ingredients in container of an electric blender; cover and process until smooth, stopping once to scrape down sides. With blender on high, gradually add gelatin. Pour into prepared crust; chill until firm.

**Arrange** oranges on top; drizzle with orange marmalade. **Yield: 10 servings.**

PER SERVING: 134 CALORIES (22% FROM FAT)
FAT 3.3G (SATURATED FAT 0.0G)
PROTEIN 5.2G CARBOHYDRATE 21.4G
CHOLESTEROL 1MG SODIUM 199MG

# Italian-Style Dinner

### Serves 2

Veal Marsala
Hearts of Romaine with Caper Vinaigrette
Italian bread (1 slice per serving)
Light Biscotti (2 slices per serving)
Coffee

*Total Calories per Serving: 467*
*(Calories from Fat: 16%)*

## Veal Marsala

6  ounces veal cutlets
2  tablespoons all-purpose flour
Olive oil-flavored vegetable cooking spray
⅓  cup Marsala wine
1  cup sliced fresh mushrooms
½  cup sweet red pepper strips
½  cup sliced onion, separated into rings
⅔  cup canned no-salt-added chicken broth
1  teaspoon lemon juice
¼  teaspoon salt
¼  teaspoon pepper
1  cup cooked fettuccine (cooked without salt
    or fat)

**Place** veal between 2 sheets of heavy-duty plastic wrap; flatten to ¼-inch thickness, using a meat mallet. Cut into 1-inch squares; dredge in flour.

**Coat** a nonstick skillet with cooking spray; place over medium-high heat until hot. Add veal to skillet; cook veal on both sides until browned.

**Transfer** veal to a lightly greased 1-quart baking dish. Deglaze pan by pouring wine into skillet; pour pan drippings over veal, and set veal aside.

**Combine** mushrooms and next 6 ingredients in skillet; cook until vegetables are tender. Spoon vegetables and pan drippings over veal.

**Bake** at 400° for 15 to 20 minutes or until mixture is bubbly. Serve veal mixture over ½ cup hot cooked fettuccine. **Yield: 2 servings.**

PER SERVING: 259 CALORIES (13% FROM FAT)
FAT 3.7G (SATURATED FAT 0.9G)
PROTEIN 22.6G CARBOHYDRATE 31.9G
CHOLESTEROL 71MG SODIUM 375MG

Veal Marsala and Hearts of Romaine

# Hearts of Romaine with Caper Vinaigrette

3 cups inner leaves of romaine lettuce
¼ cup sliced cucumber
1 slice red onion, separated into rings
Caper Vinaigrette

**Combine** first 3 ingredients; toss. Divide on 2 serving plates. Drizzle 1½ tablespoons vinaigrette over greens. **Yield: 2 (1½-cup) servings.**

## Caper Vinaigrette

1 teaspoon cornstarch
½ cup water
3 tablespoons rice vinegar
1 tablespoon low-sodium soy sauce
1 tablespoon sherry
¼ teaspoon minced fresh garlic
1 teaspoon olive oil
1 teaspoon sugar
1 tablespoon capers

**Combine** first 8 ingredients in a small saucepan; stir well. Place over medium heat; bring to a boil, stirring constantly. Cook 1 minute, stirring constantly. Remove from heat; stir in capers. Cover and chill. **Yield: ¾ cup.**

PER SERVING: 31 CALORIES (23% FROM FAT)
FAT 0.8G (SATURATED FAT 0.1G)
PROTEIN 1.7G CARBOHYDRATE 4.5G
CHOLESTEROL 0MG SODIUM 141MG

# Light Biscotti

½ cup firmly packed brown sugar
½ cup frozen egg substitute, thawed
3 tablespoons vegetable oil
1 teaspoon grated lemon rind
1 teaspoon almond extract
⅓ cup ground almonds
1¾ cups all-purpose flour
1 teaspoon baking powder
¼ teaspoon salt
Vegetable cooking spray

**Combine** first 5 ingredients in a large mixing bowl; beat at medium speed of an electric mixer until smooth. Add almonds; beat until well blended.

**Combine** flour, baking powder, and salt. Add to batter; beat until blended. Cover; chill 3 hours.

**Coat** 2 sheets of heavy-duty plastic wrap with cooking spray. Divide dough in half; shape each half into a 12-inch log on plastic wrap.

**Transfer** logs to a cookie sheet coated with cooking spray. Using floured hands, flatten logs to ½-inch thickness. Bake at 325° for 25 minutes.

**Transfer** logs to a wire rack; cool. Slice each log diagonally into ½-inch slices. Place slices, cut side down, on cookie sheets. Bake at 300° for 15 minutes or until slices are dry. Cool on wire racks (biscotti will be crisp). **Yield: 40 slices.**

PER SLICE: 47 CALORIES (33% FROM FAT)
FAT 1.7G (SATURATED FAT 0.2G)
PROTEIN 1.1G CARBOHYDRATE 7.1G
CHOLESTEROL 0MG SODIUM 20MG

## Cut the Fat—Pump Up the Flavor

- Cook with bold-flavored ingredients. Some good choices are chiles, citrus, garlic, mustard, onion, spices, and vinegar.
- Romano, Parmesan, and feta cheeses add a lot of flavor with only a little fat.
- Keep a selection of jam, jelly, and marmalade on hand. They add a strong flavor to marinades, salad dressings, fruit salsas, and basting sauces.
- Salsas can make a routine meal special. And most salsas are fat-free.

# Down-Home Delicious

Chicken Croquettes and Mushroom Sauce
Green Beans and Potatoes
Sliced tomatoes (4 slices per serving)
New-Fashioned Apple Cobbler

*Total Calories per Serving: 538
(Calories from Fat: 19%)*

## Chicken Croquettes and Mushroom Sauce

**6 (4-ounce) skinned and boned chicken breast halves**
**1 stalk celery, cut into 1-inch pieces**
**1 medium carrot, cut into 1-inch pieces**
**1 small onion, cut into ½-inch slices**
**2 cups water**
**½ cup diced celery**
**½ cup diced onion**
**Vegetable cooking spray**
**½ cup frozen egg substitute, thawed**
**½ teaspoon salt**
**½ teaspoon pepper**
**2 tablespoons cornstarch**
**½ cup skim milk**
**½ cup cracker crumbs**
**¼ teaspoon paprika**
**Mushroom Sauce**

**Combine** first 5 ingredients in a large saucepan; bring to a boil. Cover, reduce heat, and cook 15 minutes or until chicken is tender. Remove chicken from broth; strain broth, reserving 1½ cups. Set aside.

**Position** knife blade in food processor bowl. Place chicken in processor bowl; process 45 seconds or until chicken is finely chopped but not smooth. Set aside.

**Sauté** ½ cup diced celery and ½ cup diced onion in a large skillet coated with cooking spray. Remove from heat. Stir in chicken, egg substitute, salt, and pepper.

**Combine** cornstarch, milk, and ½ cup reserved broth in a small saucepan. Cook over medium heat, stirring constantly, until mixture begins to boil; boil 1 minute, stirring constantly.

**Stir** sauce into chicken mixture; shape into 6 croquettes. Combine cracker crumbs and paprika; roll croquettes in crumbs, and place on a baking sheet coated with cooking spray.

**Bake** at 375° for 30 minutes or until croquettes are thoroughly heated. Serve with ¼ cup Mushroom Sauce. **Yield: 6 servings.**

### Mushroom Sauce

**2 cups sliced fresh mushrooms**
**2 tablespoons reduced-calorie margarine, melted**
**2 tablespoons all-purpose flour**
**1 cup reserved chicken broth**
**⅛ teaspoon salt**
**¼ teaspoon pepper**

**Sauté** mushrooms in margarine in a saucepan over medium heat. Add flour, stirring until smooth. Cook 1 minute, stirring constantly.

**Stir** chicken broth gradually into mushroom mixture; cook over medium heat, stirring constantly, until thickened and bubbly. Stir in salt and pepper. **Yield 1½ cups.**

PER SERVING: 241 CALORIES (24% FROM FAT)
FAT 6.5G (SATURATED FAT 1.2G)
PROTEIN 30.1G CARBOHYDRATE 13.7G
CHOLESTEROL 71MG SODIUM 501MG

# Green Beans and Potatoes

4 medium-size red potatoes, cut into eighths
2 (16-ounce) cans no-salt-added green beans, drained
1 medium onion, sliced and separated into rings
1 teaspoon beef-flavored bouillon granules
½ teaspoon garlic powder
¼ teaspoon pepper
1 cup water

**Layer** all ingredients in a large saucepan in the order given; bring to a boil. Cover, reduce heat, and simmer 20 minutes or until potato is fork tender. **Yield: 6 (1-cup) servings.**

PER SERVING: 100 CALORIES (3% FROM FAT)
FAT 0.3G (SATURATED FAT 0.1G)
PROTEIN 3.2G CARBOHYDRATE 22.4G
CHOLESTEROL 0MG SODIUM 166MG

# New-Fashioned Apple Cobbler

1 tablespoon cornstarch
½ cup apple juice, divided
5 cups peeled and sliced cooking apple
⅓ cup firmly packed brown sugar
½ teaspoon ground cinnamon
¼ teaspoon ground nutmeg
¼ teaspoon ground cloves
Vegetable cooking spray
½ cup all-purpose flour
2 tablespoons corn oil margarine
1 to 2 tablespoons cold water

**Combine** cornstarch and ¼ cup apple juice; set aside.

**Combine** remaining ¼ cup apple juice, apple, and next 4 ingredients in a heavy saucepan; bring to a boil. Reduce heat, and simmer 10 minutes, stirring occasionally.

**Stir** in cornstarch mixture; cook over medium heat, stirring constantly, until mixture begins to boil. Boil 1 minute, stirring constantly, until mixture is thickened and bubbly.

**Remove** from heat; pour into an 8-inch square baking dish coated with cooking spray. Set aside.

**Place** flour in a small bowl; cut in margarine with a pastry blender until mixture is crumbly. Sprinkle cold water evenly over surface of mixture; stir with a fork until dry ingredients are moistened.

**Shape** dough into a ball; gently press between 2 sheets of heavy-duty plastic wrap into a 4-inch circle. Chill 15 minutes.

**Roll** dough to an 8-inch square; freeze 5 minutes. Remove top sheet of plastic wrap; cut dough into strips to fit baking dish. Arrange strips over apples in a lattice design.

**Bake** at 425° for 30 to 35 minutes or until cobbler is bubbly and crust is golden. **Yield: 6 (½-cup) servings.**

PER SERVING: 184 CALORIES (22% FROM FAT)
FAT 4.4G (SATURATED FAT 0.8G)
PROTEIN 1.2G CARBOHYDRATE 36.6G
CHOLESTEROL 0MG SODIUM 50MG

## New-Fashioned Apple Cobbler Technique

To make lattice design, lay 4 strips of pastry over filling. Weave 4 more strips over and under the first strips.

Individual Chicken Bake, Mixed Greens, and New Potato Medley

# A Family Affair

## Individual Chicken Bake

2 cups diced cooked chicken breast (skinned
   before cooking and cooked without salt)
¾ cup diced celery
¼ cup diced onion
1 (4-ounce) can sliced mushrooms, drained
1 cup evaporated skimmed milk
¼ cup frozen egg substitute, thawed
1 tablespoon low-sodium Worcestershire sauce
½ teaspoon salt
¼ teaspoon ground white pepper
Vegetable cooking spray
⅓ cup whole-berry cranberry sauce

**Combine** first 9 ingredients; divide equally into six 6-ounce custard cups coated with cooking spray. Cover loosely with aluminum foil.

**Bake** at 350° for 50 minutes or until a knife inserted in center comes out clean. Uncover and let stand 5 minutes. Remove chicken from custard cups; top each serving with cranberry sauce. **Yield: 6 servings.**

PER SERVING: 167 CALORIES (13% FROM FAT)
FAT 2.4G (SATURATED FAT 0.6G)
PROTEIN 22.3G CARBOHYDRATE 13.1G
CHOLESTEROL 50MG SODIUM 395MG

# Mixed Greens with Blue Cheese Vinaigrette

2 tablespoons water
1½ tablespoons vegetable oil
1 tablespoon white vinegar
1 tablespoon lemon juice
1 teaspoon Dijon mustard
½ teaspoon dried oregano
¼ teaspoon sugar
¼ teaspoon freshly ground pepper
1 ounce crumbled blue cheese
3 cups torn iceberg lettuce
3 cups torn romaine lettuce
2 cups torn Bibb lettuce

**Combine** first 9 ingredients in a jar; cover tightly, and shake vigorously. Chill thoroughly.

**Combine** salad greens in a large bowl; divide greens evenly among 6 serving plates.

**Drizzle** about 1 tablespoon dressing over each salad. **Yield: 6 servings.**

PER SERVING: 60 CALORIES (75% FROM FAT)
FAT 5.0G (SATURATED FAT 1.5G)
PROTEIN 2.0G CARBOHYDRATE 2.5G
CHOLESTEROL 4MG SODIUM 96MG

# New Potato Medley

1 tablespoon reduced-calorie margarine
3 cups cubed new potato
1½ cups diagonally sliced carrot
1 cup chopped onion
¼ teaspoon salt
¼ teaspoon pepper

**Melt** margarine in a saucepan over medium heat. Add potato and remaining ingredients; toss.

**Cover,** reduce heat, and cook 20 minutes, stirring once. **Yield: 6 (¾-cup) servings.**

PER SERVING: 100 CALORIES (13% FROM FAT)
FAT 1.4G (SATURATED FAT 0.0G)
PROTEIN 1.9G CARBOHYDRATE 20.9G
CHOLESTEROL 0MG SODIUM 130MG

# Baked Apples à l'Orange

6 medium-size cooking apples
¼ cup unsweetened apple juice
¼ cup water
1 tablespoon lemon juice
2 whole cloves
1 (4-inch) stick cinnamon, broken in half
⅓ cup reduced-calorie orange marmalade
6 small gingersnap cookies, crushed

**Core** apples to within ½ inch from bottom; peel top third of each apple. Place apples in an 11- x 7- x 1½-inch baking dish; add apple juice and next 4 ingredients.

**Bake,** uncovered, at 350° for 30 minutes, basting with cooking liquid. Remove from oven; spoon equal amounts of marmalade into center of each apple, and sprinkle with cookie crumbs.

**Bake** 5 additional minutes. Remove and discard cloves and cinnamon stick. **Yield: 6 servings.**

PER SERVING: 122 CALORIES (13% FROM FAT)
FAT 1.8G (SATURATED FAT 0.4G)
PROTEIN 0.8G CARBOHYDRATE 27.8G
CHOLESTEROL 3MG SODIUM 14MG

# Catfish Catch

## Oven-Fried Catfish

¾  **cup crushed cornflakes cereal**
¾  **teaspoon celery salt**
¼  **teaspoon onion powder**
¼  **teaspoon paprika**
**Dash of pepper**
4  **(6-ounce) skinless farm-raised catfish fillets,
    halved**
**Vegetable cooking spray**

Oven-Fried Catfish, Green Bean Slaw, Baked Hush Puppies, and Red Seafood Sauce

**Combine** first 5 ingredients; set aside.

**Spray** all sides of fish with cooking spray, and coat with cornflake mixture.

**Arrange** fillets in a single layer on a baking sheet coated with cooking spray. Spray tops of fillets with cooking spray.

**Bake** at 350° for 30 minutes or until fish flakes when tested with a fork. **Yield: 4 servings.**

PER SERVING: 247 CALORIES (32% FROM FAT)
FAT 8.7G (SATURATED FAT 1.6G)
PROTEIN 25.5G CARBOHYDRATE 14.0G
CHOLESTEROL 77MG SODIUM 673MG

## Red Seafood Sauce

⅔ cup no-salt-added ketchup
1 tablespoon prepared horseradish
1 tablespoon lemon juice

**Combine** all ingredients; cover and chill. Serve with fish or shellfish. **Yield: ¾ cup.**

PER TABLESPOON 14 CALORIES (0% FROM FAT)
FAT 0.0G (SATURATED FAT 0.0G)
PROTEIN 0.0G CARBOHYDRATE 3.8G
CHOLESTEROL 0MG SODIUM 7MG

## Green Bean Slaw

½ pound fresh green beans
¼ small onion, cut into thin strips
   (about ¼ cup)
½ cup thin sweet red pepper strips
1 medium cucumber, peeled, seeded, and cut
   into thin strips
2½ tablespoons tarragon vinegar or other
   herb vinegar
2 tablespoons nonfat process cream cheese
1 tablespoon skim milk
1 teaspoon sugar
¼ teaspoon salt
¼ teaspoon pepper

**Wash** beans; remove ends. Cook in boiling water 8 minutes or until crisp-tender; drain. Plunge into ice water to stop cooking process; drain.

**Combine** beans, onion, sweet red pepper, and cucumber; toss gently, and set aside.

**Combine** vinegar and next 5 ingredients, stirring until smooth. Pour dressing over bean mixture; toss gently. Cover and chill thoroughly before serving. **Yield: 4 (1-cup) servings.**

PER SERVING: 49 CALORIES (4% FROM FAT)
FAT 0.2G (SATURATED FAT 0.5G)
PROTEIN 3.7G CARBOHYDRATE 9.1G
CHOLESTEROL 3MG SODIUM 241MG

## Baked Hush Puppies

1 cup yellow cornmeal
1 cup all-purpose flour
1 tablespoon baking powder
1 teaspoon salt
1 teaspoon sugar
⅛ teaspoon ground red pepper
2 large eggs, lightly beaten
¾ cup milk
¼ cup vegetable oil
½ cup finely chopped onion
Vegetable cooking spray

**Combine** first 6 ingredients in a large bowl; make a well in center of mixture. Set aside.

**Combine** eggs and next 3 ingredients, stirring well; add to dry mixture, stirring just until dry ingredients are moistened.

**Coat** miniature muffin pans with cooking spray. Spoon about 1 tablespoon batter into each cup. (Cups will be about three-fourths full.)

**Bake** at 425° for 15 minutes or until done. Serve immediately. **Yield: 3 dozen.**

PER HUSH PUPPY: 55 CALORIES (39% FROM FAT)
FAT 2.4G (SATURATED FAT 0.2G)
PROTEIN 1.3G CARBOHYDRATE 6.9G
CHOLESTEROL 13MG SODIUM 71MG

# Dinner from the Orient

## Hot-and-Sour Soup

2 (14¼-ounce) cans no-salt-added chicken broth
½ cup sliced fresh mushrooms
1 teaspoon minced fresh gingerroot
1 (4-ounce) skinned and boned chicken breast
   half, cut into thin strips
⅓ cup canned bamboo shoots, cut into strips
3 tablespoons rice vinegar
3 tablespoons low-sodium soy sauce
¼ teaspoon hot sauce
⅛ teaspoon pepper
1 egg white, lightly beaten
¼ cup sliced green onions
¼ cup fresh snow pea pods
1 tablespoon cornstarch
¼ cup water

**Combine** first 3 ingredients in a 2-quart saucepan; bring to a boil. Add chicken; simmer 10 minutes. Add bamboo shoots; simmer 5 minutes.

**Add** vinegar and next 3 ingredients; return to a boil. Slowly pour egg white into soup, stirring constantly. (The egg white forms lacy strands as it cooks.) Stir in green onions and snow peas.

**Combine** cornstarch and water in a small bowl. Add to soup, and return to a boil; boil 1 minute, stirring gently. **Yield: 4 (1-cup) servings.**

PER SERVING: 76 CALORIES (5% FROM FAT)
FAT 0.4G (SATURATED FAT 0.1G)
PROTEIN 8.5G CARBOHYDRATE 5.2G
CHOLESTEROL 16MG SODIUM 334MG

## Orange Roughy and Vegetable Stir-Fry

Vegetable cooking spray
2 teaspoons vegetable oil
1 tablespoon peeled, minced fresh gingerroot
1 clove garlic, sliced
1 pound orange roughy, cut into 1-inch cubes
1 medium onion, cut into thin wedges
2 cups sliced fresh broccoli
1 cup sliced fresh mushrooms
1 large sweet red pepper, cut into strips
1 teaspoon cornstarch
2 tablespoons water
2 tablespoons dry white wine
2 tablespoons low-sodium soy sauce
¼ teaspoon hot sauce
4 cups hot cooked rice (cooked without salt
   or fat)

**Coat** a wok or large nonstick skillet with cooking spray; add oil, and heat at medium-high (375°) for 2 minutes. Add gingerroot and garlic; stir-fry 2 to 3 minutes.

**Add** orange roughy, and stir-fry just until fish is cooked. Remove fish from wok; let wok cool.

**Coat** wok with cooking spray; add onion, and stir-fry 1 minute. Add broccoli, mushrooms, and sweet red pepper; stir-fry 3 minutes or until broccoli is crisp-tender. Stir fish into vegetables.

**Combine** cornstarch and water; stir in wine, soy sauce, and hot sauce. Pour over fish, and stir-fry until thickened and bubbly. Serve over rice.
**Yield: 4 servings.**

PER SERVING: 360 CALORIES (10% FROM FAT)
FAT 3.8G (SATURATED FAT 0.5G)
PROTEIN 23.4G CARBOHYDRATE 57.2G
CHOLESTEROL 23MG SODIUM 331MG

# Almond Cookies

½ **cup margarine, softened**
¼ **cup sugar**
1 **egg yolk**
1 **tablespoon water**
½ **teaspoon almond extract**
1¼ **cups all-purpose flour**

**Beat** softened margarine and sugar at medium speed of an electric mixer until light and fluffy. Add egg yolk, water, and almond extract; beat well. Stir in flour.

**Use** a cookie press or decorator pastry bag fitted with a bar disc to shape dough into long strips; cut strips into 2-inch pieces.

**Place** dough on ungreased cookie sheets; bake at 400° for 6 minutes or until lightly browned. Remove from cookie sheets, and cool completely on wire racks. Store in an airtight container. **Yield: 4 dozen.**

PER COOKIE: 33 CALORIES (55% FROM FAT)
FAT 2.0G (SATURATED FAT 0.4G)
PROTEIN 0.4G CARBOHYDRATE 3.4G
CHOLESTEROL 5MG SODIUM 22MG

Orange Roughy and Vegetable Stir-Fry, Hot-and-Sour Soup, and Almond Cookies

# Papillote Surprise

## Shrimp Cancun en Papillote

**10  ounces unpeeled medium-size fresh shrimp**
**Vegetable cooking spray**
**¾  cup chunky salsa, divided**
**½  cup (2 ounces) shredded part-skim**
   **mozzarella cheese**
**3  whole ripe olives, sliced**

**Peel** shrimp, and devein, if desired. Cut two 15- x 12-inch pieces of parchment paper or aluminum foil; fold in half lengthwise. Trim each into a heart shape. Place hearts on a baking sheet. Coat one side of each with cooking spray.

**Divide** shrimp equally, and place on sides of hearts coated with cooking spray. Top each with ¼ cup salsa.

**Fold** over remaining half of paper or foil. Pleat and crimp edges together to seal. Twist end slightly to seal.

**Bake** at 400° for 10 to 12 minutes or until parchment is puffed and lightly browned. Cut an X in top of paper, and top each with cheese and olives. Bake 1 minute or until cheese melts. Serve with ¼ cup salsa. **Yield: 2 servings.**

Per Serving: 215 Calories (32% from Fat)
Fat 7.6g (Saturated Fat 3.4g)
Protein 29.5g  Carbohydrate 6.6g
Cholesterol 178mg  Sodium 575mg

## Stuffed Scalloped Tomatoes

**2  medium tomatoes (¾ pound)**
**Vegetable cooking spray**
**2  tablespoons diced onion**
**½  teaspoon brown sugar**
**¼  teaspoon salt**
**¼  teaspoon pepper**
**⅔  cup soft breadcrumbs, toasted**
**1  tablespoon grated Parmesan cheese**

**Cut** tops from tomatoes; chop tops, and set aside. Scoop out pulp, leaving shells intact. Reserve pulp.

**Coat** a nonstick skillet with cooking spray; place over medium-high heat until hot. Add onion, and sauté until tender.

**Add** chopped tomato tops, reserved tomato pulp, brown sugar, and next 3 ingredients; stir well, and remove from heat.

**Spoon** stuffing mixture into tomato shells, and place in an 8-inch square baking dish coated with cooking spray. Sprinkle with Parmesan cheese, and bake at 350° for 10 minutes or until thoroughly heated. **Yield: 2 servings.**

Per Serving: 88 Calories (20% from Fat)
Fat 2.0g (Saturated Fat 0.7g)
Protein 3.5g  Carbohydrate 15.2g
Cholesterol 2mg  Sodium 428mg

### Steaming Vegetables

For the steamed vegetables, pair 1 cup julienne-sliced zucchini with ½ cup julienne-sliced carrot; toss with 1 teaspoon reduced-calorie margarine and ½ teaspoon lemon-pepper seasoning.

Shrimp Cancun en Papillote

# Shrimp en Brochette

## Shrimp with Peanut Sauce

2 tablespoons sliced green onions
2 cloves garlic, minced
Vegetable cooking spray
¾ cup no-salt-added chicken broth
3 tablespoons creamy peanut butter
1 tablespoon reduced-sodium soy sauce
1 tablespoon lemon juice
1 teaspoon chili powder
1 teaspoon brown sugar
½ teaspoon ground ginger
1 pound unpeeled large fresh shrimp

**Cook** green onions and garlic in a skillet coated with cooking spray over medium heat, stirring constantly, about 3 minutes.

**Add** chicken broth and next 6 ingredients, stirring until smooth. Reduce heat, and simmer 10 minutes, stirring often. Remove from heat; cool.

**Peel** shrimp, leaving tails attached. Place shrimp in sauce; turn to coat. Cover and chill 1 hour. Remove from sauce; discard sauce.

**Thread** shrimp onto skewers. Broil 6 inches from heat (with electric oven door partially opened) 5 minutes on each side or until shrimp turn pink. **Yield: 4 servings.**

PER SERVING: 146 CALORIES (28% FROM FAT)
FAT 4.5G (SATURATED FAT 0.8G)
PROTEIN 22.6G CARBOHYDRATE 3.0G
CHOLESTEROL 156MG SODIUM 231MG

## Herbed Vegetables

1 cup broccoli flowerets
1 cup diagonally cut, 2-inch-long asparagus pieces
½ cup (2- x ½-inch) pieces sweet red pepper
½ cup (2- x ½-inch) pieces sweet yellow pepper
½ cup sliced fresh mushrooms
1 tablespoon chopped fresh marjoram
1 teaspoon chopped fresh oregano or ¼ teaspoon dried oregano
½ teaspoon chopped fresh rosemary
¼ teaspoon salt
⅛ teaspoon pepper
1 tablespoon water
1 tablespoon reduced-calorie margarine

**Combine** all ingredients in a 1½-quart microwave-safe baking dish. Cover tightly with heavy-duty plastic wrap; fold back a small edge of wrap to allow steam to escape.

**Microwave** at HIGH 3½ minutes or until crisp-tender, stirring once. **Yield: 4 (⅔-cup) servings.**

PER SERVING: 42 CALORIES (39% FROM FAT)
FAT 1.8G (SATURATED FAT 0.3G)
PROTEIN 2.4G CARBOHYDRATE 5.6G
CHOLESTEROL 0MG SODIUM 194MG

### Shrimp Secrets

• Fresh raw shrimp vary in color from greenish gray to pink, indicating the type of water the shrimp came from, not their quality. All shrimp will turn pink during cooking.

• To devein shrimp, cut a shallow slit down the middle of the outside curve. Remove dark vein; rinse with water.

Pumpkin Cake

# Pumpkin Cake

2¾ cups all-purpose flour
1 teaspoon baking soda
½ teaspoon baking powder
¼ teaspoon salt
1 teaspoon ground nutmeg
1 teaspoon ground cloves
1 teaspoon ground cinnamon
3 large eggs, lightly beaten
2 cups sugar
1 cup unsweetened applesauce
1 (16-ounce) can pumpkin
1 cup raisins, chopped
½ cup chopped pecans
Vegetable cooking spray
1 teaspoon powdered sugar
1 cup reduced-calorie frozen whipped
   topping, thawed

**Combine** first 7 ingredients in a large bowl; make a well in center of mixture.

**Combine** eggs and next 3 ingredients; add to dry ingredients, stirring just until moistened. Fold in raisins and pecans. Spoon into a 12-cup Bundt pan coated with cooking spray.

**Bake** at 350° for 1 hour and 10 minutes or until a wooden pick inserted in center comes out clean.

**Cool** in pan on a wire rack 10 minutes; remove from pan, and cool completely on wire rack.

**Sprinkle** with powdered sugar. Dollop 1 tablespoon whipped topping on each slice. **Yield: 16 servings.**

PER SERVING: 269 CALORIES (15% FROM FAT)
FAT 4.5G (SATURATED FAT 0.6G)
PROTEIN 4.5G CARBOHYDRATE 54.8G
CHOLESTEROL 41MG SODIUM 98MG

# Vegetarian Supper

───── **Serves 8** ─────

Spinach-Bean Lasagna
Tomato-Cucumber Salad with Yogurt-Herb Dressing
Italian rolls (1 per serving)
Lemon sorbet (½ cup per serving)

*Total Calories per Serving: 647*
*(Calories from Fat: 18%)*

## Spinach-Bean Lasagna

2 (15-ounce) cans kidney beans, rinsed and
   drained
1¾ cups water
1 (27.5-ounce) jar reduced-fat, reduced-
   sodium pasta sauce
1 (10-ounce) package frozen chopped spinach,
   thawed and well drained
1 (15-ounce) container part-skim ricotta
   cheese
¼ cup frozen egg substitute, thawed
Vegetable cooking spray
10 lasagna noodles, uncooked
1 cup (4 ounces) shredded part-skim
   mozzarella cheese
¼ cup grated Parmesan cheese

**Position** knife blade in food processor bowl;
add beans. Pulse 2 or 3 times; gradually add
water, and pulse until beans are coarsely chopped.

**Combine** bean mixture and pasta sauce in a
saucepan; bring to a boil. Reduce heat, and simmer, stirring occasionally, 10 minutes; set aside.

**Combine** spinach, ricotta cheese, and egg substitute; set aside.

**Coat** a 13- x 9- x 2-inch baking dish with
cooking spray, and spread a thin layer of sauce on
bottom of dish.

**Arrange** 5 noodles over sauce. Spread half of
spinach mixture over noodles; top with mozzarella.

Spoon half of sauce over cheese. Repeat layers.

**Cover** and chill 24 hours. Remove from refrigerator, and let stand at room temperature 30 minutes.

**Cover** and bake at 350° for 1 hour. Uncover
and sprinkle with Parmesan cheese; bake 15
additional minutes. **Yield: 8 servings.**

PER SERVING: 436 CALORIES (22% FROM FAT)
FAT 10.8G (SATURATED FAT 4.7G)
PROTEIN 24.8G CARBOHYDRATE 62.2G
CHOLESTEROL 27MG SODIUM 364MG

## Tomato-Cucumber Salad with Yogurt-Herb Dressing

1 head Boston lettuce
4 small tomatoes, cut into wedges
1 medium cucumber, scored and sliced
½ small purple onion, sliced and separated
   into rings
**Yogurt-Herb Dressing**

**Line** individual plates with lettuce leaves;
arrange tomato, cucumber, and onion in pin-
wheel fashion on plates.

**Top** with 2 tablespoons Yogurt-Herb Dressing.
**Yield: 8 servings.**

### Yogurt-Herb Dressing
¾ cup plain nonfat yogurt
¼ cup nonfat mayonnaise
1 teaspoon chopped fresh dillweed
1 teaspoon chopped fresh chives
⅛ teaspoon white pepper

**Combine** all ingredients; cover and chill.
**Yield: 1 cup.**

PER SERVING: 41 CALORIES (7% FROM FAT)
FAT 0.3G (SATURATED FAT 0.1G)
PROTEIN 2.3G CARBOHYDRATE 8.2G
CHOLESTEROL 0MG SODIUM 119MG

Spinach-Bean Lasagna and Tomato-Cucumber Salad with Yogurt-Herb Dressing

# Simple Supper

(pictured on page 11)

---

**Serves 8**

Bean and Cornbread Casserole
Apple-Carrot Slaw
Yogurt with Mocha Sauce
(recipe on page 129)

*Total Calories per Serving: 552*
*(Calories from Fat: 12%)*

---

## Bean and Cornbread Casserole

Vegetable cooking spray
1  cup chopped onion
½  cup chopped green pepper
2  cloves garlic, minced
1  (16-ounce) can kidney beans, drained
1  (16-ounce) can pinto beans, drained
1  (16-ounce) can no-salt-added tomatoes,
    undrained and chopped
1  (8-ounce) can no-salt-added tomato sauce
1  teaspoon chili powder
½  teaspoon pepper
½  teaspoon prepared mustard
⅛  teaspoon hot sauce
1  cup yellow cornmeal
1  cup all-purpose flour
2½  teaspoons baking powder
½  teaspoon salt
1  tablespoon sugar
1¼  cups skim milk
½  cup frozen egg substitute, thawed
3  tablespoons vegetable oil
1  (8½-ounce) can no-salt-added, cream-style
    corn
Garnish: green pepper strips

**Coat** a large nonstick skillet with cooking
spray; place over medium-high heat until hot. Add
onion, chopped green pepper, and garlic; cook,
stirring constantly, until vegetables are tender.

**Stir** in kidney beans and next 7 ingredients.
Cover and cook 5 minutes; spoon into a 13- x 9-
x 2-inch baking dish coated with cooking spray.
Set aside.

**Combine** cornmeal and next 4 ingredients in a
medium bowl. Combine milk and next 3 ingredients; add to dry mixture, stirring until dry ingredients are moistened. Spoon evenly over bean
mixture to within 1 inch of edges of dish.

**Bake** at 375° for 30 to 35 minutes or until
cornbread is done. Cut into 8 squares. Garnish, if
desired. **Yield: 8 servings.**

PER SERVING: 343 CALORIES (16% FROM FAT)
FAT 6.2G (SATURATED FAT 1.1G)
PROTEIN 13.5G CARBOHYDRATE 59.5G
CHOLESTEROL 1MG SODIUM 380MG

## Apple-Carrot Slaw

4  cups shredded cabbage
2  cups shredded carrot
1¾  cups unpeeled, chopped Red Delicious
    apple
⅔  cup fat-free mayonnaise
2  tablespoons sugar
⅓  cup white vinegar
1  teaspoon celery seeds
8  cabbage leaves (optional)

**Combine** first 3 ingredients in a large bowl.
Combine mayonnaise and next 3 ingredients;
pour over cabbage mixture, tossing gently to
coat. Cover and chill. Serve on cabbage leaves, if
desired. **Yield: 8 (1-cup) servings.**

PER SERVING: 64 CALORIES (3% FROM FAT)
FAT 0.2G (SATURATED FAT 0.0G)
PROTEIN 0.8G CARBOHYDRATE 15.9G
CHOLESTEROL 0MG SODIUM 267MG

# Souper Suppers

Whether you simmer a pot of soup for hours or just heat the ingredients, soup is hard to beat. You can serve it with a healthful salad or a hearty sandwich—even when you're eating light.

French Market Soup, Cornmeal Yeast Muffins, Creamy Coleslaw

Bean and Turkey Soup, Potato-Corn Chowder, Warm Chocolate Pudding Cake

Chocolate-Kahlúa Brownies, Chicken and Sausage Gumbo, Gazpacho Molded Salad

Chicken, Artichoke, and Mushroom Soup, Parsley-Garlic Rolls

Roasted Pepper and Chicken Soup (complete menu on page 38)

French Market Soup and Cornmeal Yeast Muffin

# Soup for the Family

## French Market Soup

1  (12-ounce) package dried bean soup mix
9  cups water
1  cup cubed reduced-fat, reduced-salt cooked ham
¼  teaspoon ground white pepper
1  (16-ounce) can no-salt-added whole tomatoes, chopped and undrained
1½  cups chopped onion
¾  cup chopped celery
2  large cloves garlic, minced
3  tablespoons lemon juice
1  teaspoon hot sauce

Sort and wash bean soup mix; place in a Dutch oven. Cover with water 2 inches above beans; let soak 8 hours.

Drain beans, and return to Dutch oven. Add 9 cups water, ham, and white pepper. Bring to a boil; reduce heat, and simmer, uncovered, 2 hours or until beans are tender.

Add tomatoes and remaining ingredients to Dutch oven. Simmer 30 minutes, stirring occasionally. **Yield: 6 (1¼-cup) servings.**

PER SERVING: 263 CALORIES (8% FROM FAT)
FAT 2.2G (SATURATED FAT 0.7G)
PROTEIN 19.7G CARBOHYDRATE 43.5G
CHOLESTEROL 15MG SODIUM 270MG

## Cornmeal Yeast Muffins

1 package dry yeast
¼ cup warm water (105° to 115°)
1¾ cups skim milk
⅓ cup sugar
¼ cup vegetable oil
¼ cup reduced-calorie margarine
1 teaspoon salt
½ cup frozen egg substitute, thawed
1½ cups plain cornmeal
5 to 5½ cups all-purpose flour, divided
Butter-flavored vegetable cooking spray

Dissolve yeast in warm water in a large bowl; let stand 5 minutes.

Combine milk and next 4 ingredients in a saucepan; cook over low heat until margarine melts. Cool to 105° to 115°.

Add milk mixture to yeast mixture. Stir in egg substitute, cornmeal, and 2 cups flour. Beat at medium speed of an electric mixer until smooth. Stir in enough remaining flour to make a soft dough.

Turn dough out onto a lightly floured surface, and knead until smooth and elastic (about 8 minutes). Place in a bowl coated with cooking spray, turning to grease top.

Cover and let rise in a warm place (85°), free from drafts, 1 hour or until doubled in bulk.

Punch dough down; shape into 72 balls. Place 2 balls in each muffin cup coated with cooking spray. Let rise in a warm place, free from drafts, 45 minutes or until doubled in bulk.

Bake at 375° for 12 to 15 minutes or until golden. Coat muffins with cooking spray; remove from pans immediately. (These muffins freeze well.) **Yield: 3 dozen.**

PER MUFFIN: 116 CALORIES (20% FROM FAT)
FAT 2.6G (SATURATED FAT 0.4G)
PROTEIN 3.0G CARBOHYDRATE 19.8G
CHOLESTEROL 0MG SODIUM 89MG

## Jicama-Fruit Compote

1½ cups diced jicama
1½ tablespoons sugar
1½ teaspoons lemon juice
3 (2-inch) sticks cinnamon
⅓ cup orange juice
3 cups unpeeled sliced apple
¾ cup frozen pitted dark sweet cherries, thawed
⅛ teaspoon dried orange peel

Combine first 5 ingredients in a medium saucepan; cover and cook over medium heat about 10 minutes.

Add apple and remaining ingredients; cook 2 to 3 minutes. Remove and discard cinnamon sticks. Serve warm. **Yield: 6 (½-cup) servings.**

PER SERVING: 70 CALORIES (4% FROM FAT)
FAT 0.3G (SATURATED FAT 0.1G)
PROTEIN 0.6G CARBOHYDRATE 17.7G
CHOLESTEROL 0MG SODIUM 2MG

Chicken and Sausage Gumbo

# Fireside Supper

### — Serves 8 —

Chicken and Sausage Gumbo
Romaine salad (1½ cups salad and 2 tablespoons fat-free dressing per serving)
French bread (1 slice per serving)
Chocolate-Kahlúa Brownies (1 per serving)

*Total Calories per Serving: 625*
*(Calories from Fat: 22%)*

# Chicken and Sausage Gumbo

¾ cup all-purpose flour
½ pound 80% fat-free smoked sausage, cut into ¼-inch slices
Vegetable cooking spray
6 (6-ounce) skinned chicken breast halves
1 cup chopped onion
½ cup chopped green pepper
½ cup sliced celery
2 quarts hot water
3 cloves garlic, minced
2 bay leaves
2 teaspoons reduced-sodium Cajun seasoning
½ teaspoon dried thyme
1 tablespoon low-sodium Worcestershire sauce
1 teaspoon hot sauce
½ cup sliced green onions
4 cups cooked rice (cooked without salt or fat)

**Place** flour in a 13- x 9- x 2-inch pan. Bake at 400° for 15 minutes or until caramel colored, stirring flour every 5 minutes.

**Brown** sausage over medium heat in a Dutch oven coated with cooking spray. Drain and pat dry with paper towels; wipe drippings from Dutch oven.

**Brown** chicken; drain and pat dry. Wipe drippings from Dutch oven.

**Cook** onion, green pepper, and celery in Dutch oven coated with cooking spray until tender; sprinkle with browned flour. Gradually stir in water; bring to a boil.

**Add** chicken, garlic, and next 5 ingredients to Dutch oven. Reduce heat, and simmer, uncovered, 1 hour.

**Remove** chicken; cool. Add sausage, and cook gumbo, uncovered, 30 minutes. Stir in green onions; cook, uncovered, 30 additional minutes.

**Bone** chicken, and cut into strips. Add to gumbo, and cook until heated. Remove and discard bay leaves; serve gumbo over rice. **Yield: 8 (1-cup) servings.**

**Note:** For reduced-sodium Cajun seasoning, we used Tony Chachere's More Spice Less Salt Cajun blend of spices.

Per serving: 336 Calories (24% from Fat)
Fat 8.8g (Saturated Fat 3.4g)
Protein 27.4g Carbohydrate 35.1g
Cholesterol 69mg Sodium 200mg

# Chocolate-Kahlúa Brownies

1½ cups sugar
½ cup frozen egg substitute, thawed
3 tablespoons Kahlúa or other coffee-flavored liqueur
¼ cup margarine, melted
1¼ cups sifted cake flour
½ cup cocoa
1 teaspoon baking powder
½ cup finely chopped walnuts
Vegetable cooking spray

**Combine** first 4 ingredients in a large mixing bowl, stirring well. Set aside.

**Combine** flour, cocoa, and baking powder; stir into sugar mixture. Fold in walnuts.

**Spoon** batter into a 9-inch square pan coated with cooking spray.

**Bake** at 325° for 30 to 35 minutes or until a wooden pick inserted in center comes out clean. Cool in pan on a wire rack; cut into squares. **Yield: 16 servings.**

Per Serving: 177 Calories (28% from Fat)
Fat 5.5g (Saturated Fat 0.9g)
Protein 3.2g Carbohydrate 28.1g
Cholesterol 0mg Sodium 46mg

# Late Night Gathering

(pictured on page 33)

―――― Serves 6 ――――

Roasted Pepper and Chicken Soup
Spinach-Orange Salad
Spicy Cornbread Muffins (1 per serving)
Apricot Sponge Torte

*Total Calories per Serving: 497*
*(Calories from Fat: 27%)*

## Roasted Pepper and Chicken Soup

4  large sweet red peppers
4  large sweet yellow peppers
2  large green peppers
Vegetable cooking spray
1  tablespoon olive oil
4  (4-ounce) skinned and boned chicken breast
     halves
5  (10½-ounce) cans low-sodium chicken broth
½  teaspoon salt
¼  teaspoon pepper
½  teaspoon dried basil
½  teaspoon dried marjoram

**Wash** and dry peppers; place on a baking sheet, and broil 4 inches from heat (with electric oven door partially opened) 3 to 4 minutes on each side. Put peppers in a heavy-duty plastic bag; close tightly, and let stand 10 minutes to allow steam to loosen skins.

**Peel** peppers; remove and discard core and seeds. Cut peppers into 2- x ¼-inch strips, and set aside.

**Coat** a large nonstick skillet with cooking spray; add olive oil, and place over medium-high heat until hot. Add chicken, and cook 6 minutes on each side or until golden. Remove chicken from skillet, and cool slightly; cut into thin strips, and set aside.

**Add** pepper strips to skillet, and cook 2 to 3 minutes or just until tender, stirring often.

**Bring** chicken broth to a boil in a large Dutch oven. Add salt, pepper, basil, marjoram, chicken, and peppers; simmer at least 5 minutes. To serve, ladle into individual soup bowls. **Yield: 6 (1¾-cup) servings.**

PER SERVING: 176 CALORIES (29% FROM FAT)
FAT 5.7G (SATURATED FAT 0.7G)
PROTEIN 21.2G CARBOHYDRATE 10.8G
CHOLESTEROL 44MG SODIUM 332MG

## Spinach-Orange Salad

2  tablespoons orange juice
2  tablespoons white wine vinegar
1  tablespoon vegetable oil
1  tablespoon honey
¼  teaspoon grated orange rind
6  cups torn spinach
2  oranges, peeled, seeded, and sectioned
1  small purple onion, sliced and separated
     into rings
1  tablespoon pine nuts, toasted

**Combine** orange juice, vinegar, oil, honey, and orange rind in a jar; cover tightly, and shake vigorously. Chill thoroughly.

Combine spinach, orange sections, and onion rings in a salad bowl. Drizzle dressing over spinach mixture; toss gently. Sprinkle with pine nuts before serving. **Yield: 6 servings.**

PER SERVING: 79 CALORIES (39% FROM FAT)
FAT 3.4G (SATURATED FAT 0.6G)
PROTEIN 2.6G CARBOHYDRATE 11.6G
CHOLESTEROL 0MG SODIUM 46MG

## Spicy Cornbread Muffins

1½ cups yellow cornmeal
1 teaspoon baking soda
1 teaspoon sugar
½ teaspoon salt
2 egg whites
¼ cup picante sauce
3 tablespoons vegetable oil
1 (8-ounce) carton plain nonfat yogurt
Vegetable cooking spray

Combine first 4 ingredients in a large bowl; make a well in center of mixture.

Combine egg whites and next 3 ingredients; add to dry ingredients, stirring just until dry ingredients are moistened.

Spoon into muffin pans coated with cooking spray, filling two-thirds full. Bake at 425° for 18 to 20 minutes. Remove from pans. **Yield: 1 dozen.**

PER MUFFIN: 111 CALORIES (32% FROM FAT)
FAT 3.9G (SATURATED FAT 0.7G)
PROTEIN 3.2G CARBOHYDRATE 15.6G
CHOLESTEROL 0MG SODIUM 246MG

## Apricot Sponge Torte

Vegetable cooking spray
2 large eggs
¼ cup sugar
½ teaspoon vanilla extract
½ teaspoon almond extract
⅓ cup sifted cake flour
½ teaspoon baking powder
Dash of salt
1 (16-ounce) can apricot halves in light syrup, undrained
1 teaspoon cornstarch

Coat a 9-inch torte pan with removable bottom with cooking spray, and set aside.

Beat eggs at medium speed of an electric mixer until foamy. Gradually add sugar, 1 tablespoon at a time, beating until soft peaks form and sugar dissolves (about 10 minutes). Gently stir in extracts.

Combine cake flour, baking powder, and salt; fold into egg mixture. Spoon into prepared pan.

Bake at 325° for 25 minutes. Remove torte from oven.

Drain apricots, reserving ⅔ cup syrup; set aside. Arrange apricot halves, cut side down, around outside edge and center of torte. Combine cornstarch and reserved syrup in a small saucepan. Cook over medium heat, stirring constantly, until mixture boils. Cook 1 additional minute; remove from heat.

Spoon sauce over apricots. Return torte to oven, and bake 5 additional minutes or until torte pulls away from sides of pan.

Cool torte on a wire rack 5 minutes; remove outside rim from pan. Serve warm. **Yield: 6 servings.**

PER SERVING: 131 CALORIES (13% FROM FAT)
FAT 1.9G (SATURATED FAT 0.5G)
PROTEIN 3.0G CARBOHYDRATE 25.8G
CHOLESTEROL 71MG SODIUM 46MG

# Busy Day Supper

## Chicken, Artichoke, and Mushroom Soup

3 (4-ounce) skinned and boned chicken breast
   halves
2½ cups water
Vegetable cooking spray
¾ cup chopped onion
½ cup chopped celery
3 (10½-ounce) cans low-sodium chicken broth
1 bay leaf
½ teaspoon salt
½ teaspoon pepper
Dash of ground nutmeg
¾ cup thinly sliced fresh mushrooms
1 (14-ounce) can artichoke hearts, drained
   and chopped
¼ cup freshly grated Parmesan cheese

**Combine** chicken and water in a large Dutch oven; bring to a boil. Cover, reduce heat, and simmer 20 minutes or until tender.

**Remove** chicken from broth; cool slightly, and shred. Reserve broth.

**Coat** Dutch oven with cooking spray; place over medium-high heat until hot. Add onion and celery; cook, stirring constantly, until crisp-tender.

**Add** reserved chicken broth, canned chicken broth, and next 4 ingredients. Bring to a boil; cover, reduce heat, and simmer 15 minutes.

**Add** mushrooms, and cook 10 minutes. Add chicken and artichokes; cook until heated. Remove and discard bay leaf. Top each serving with cheese. **Yield: 6 (1-cup) servings.**

PER SERVING: 132 CALORIES (20% FROM FAT)
FAT 3.0G (SATURATED FAT 1.2G)
PROTEIN 17.9G CARBOHYDRATE 9.0G
CHOLESTEROL 36MG SODIUM 392MG

## Gazpacho Molded Salad

2 envelopes unflavored gelatin
¼ cup cold water
1½ cups no-salt-added vegetable juice
¼ cup red wine vinegar
¼ teaspoon hot sauce
1 clove garlic, minced
¼ cup fat-free mayonnaise
1 cup finely chopped cucumber
½ cup finely chopped green pepper
½ cup finely chopped onion
Vegetable cooking spray
6 lettuce leaves
Garnish: cucumber slices

**Sprinkle** gelatin over cold water in a medium saucepan; let stand 1 minute. Add vegetable juice and next 3 ingredients. Cook over medium heat, stirring until gelatin dissolves (about 2 minutes).

**Add** mayonnaise; whisk until blended. Chill until the consistency of unbeaten egg white.

**Fold** in cucumber, green pepper, and onion; spoon into six ½-cup molds lightly coated with cooking spray.

**Cover** and chill 8 hours. Unmold onto lettuce leaves; garnish, if desired. **Yield: 6 servings.**

PER SERVING: 46 CALORIES (8% FROM FAT)
FAT 0.4G (SATURATED FAT 0.0G)
PROTEIN 3.3G CARBOHYDRATE 7.7G
CHOLESTEROL 0MG SODIUM 146MG

Chicken, Artichoke, and Mushroom Soup and Gazpacho Molded Salad

# Warm Chocolate Pudding Cake

1  **cup all-purpose flour**
2  **teaspoons baking powder**
⅛  **teaspoon salt**
½  **cup sugar**
2  **tablespoons unsweetened cocoa**
**Vegetable cooking spray**
½  **cup skim milk**
3  **tablespoons reduced-calorie margarine, melted**
1  **teaspoon vanilla extract**
¼  **cup sugar**
¼  **cup firmly packed brown sugar**
¼  **cup unsweetened cocoa**
1½  **cups warm water**
**Vanilla low-fat ice cream**

**Combine** first 5 ingredients in a 9-inch square pan coated with cooking spray; stir in milk, margarine, and vanilla. Spread evenly in pan.

**Combine** ¼ cup sugar, brown sugar, and ¼ cup cocoa; sprinkle evenly over batter. Pour warm water over top. Bake at 350° for 30 minutes. Spoon into individual dishes. Top each serving with ¼ cup ice cream. **Yield: 8 servings.**

PER SERVING: 241 CALORIES (19% FROM FAT)
FAT 5.0G (SATURATED FAT 1.6G)
PROTEIN 4.6G CARBOHYDRATE 45.7G
CHOLESTEROL 5MG SODIUM 118MG

Bean and Turkey Soup, Creamy Coleslaw, and Parsley-Garlic Rolls

# Winter Warm-Up

### Serves 6

Bean and Turkey Soup
Creamy Coleslaw
Parsley-Garlic Rolls (1 per serving)

*Total Calories per Serving: 472*
*(Calories from Fat: 13%)*

# Bean and Turkey Soup

2 cups chopped cooked turkey breast
2 cups peeled, chopped tomato
1 cup canned red kidney beans, drained and rinsed
1 cup canned pinto beans, drained and rinsed
1 cup canned black beans, drained and rinsed
1 cup canned garbanzo beans, drained and rinsed
1 cup frozen whole kernel corn
1 cup chopped onion
2 jalapeño peppers, seeded and chopped
2 cloves garlic, minced
2 (14½-ounce) cans ready-to-serve no-salt-added chicken broth
1 (12-ounce) can light beer
3 tablespoons chili powder
2 tablespoons curry powder
1 teaspoon dried basil
1 teaspoon dried oregano
1 teaspoon dried thyme
¼ teaspoon pepper
3 tablespoons reduced-sodium soy sauce
2 tablespoons Worcestershire sauce

**Combine** all ingredients in a large Dutch oven; bring to a boil over medium heat. Reduce heat; simmer, uncovered, 2 hours, stirring occasionally. **Yield: 6 (1½-cup) servings.**

PER SERVING: 338 CALORIES (11% FROM FAT)
FAT 4.1G (SATURATED FAT 0.8G)
PROTEIN 27.3G CARBOHYDRATE 46.5G
CHOLESTEROL 32MG SODIUM 649MG

# Creamy Coleslaw

6 cups shredded cabbage
¼ cup chopped green onions
⅛ teaspoon pepper
Creamy Dressing
Lettuce leaves

**Combine** first 3 ingredients in a bowl; stir in Creamy Dressing. Cover and chill at least 1 hour. Serve over lettuce. **Yield: 6 (1-cup) servings.**

## Creamy Dressing

¼ cup plain nonfat yogurt
¼ cup nonfat mayonnaise
2 tablespoons rice wine vinegar
2 teaspoons spicy brown mustard

**Combine** all ingredients; mix well. **Yield: ⅔ cup.**

PER SERVING: 36 CALORIES (8% FROM FAT)
FAT 0.3G (SATURATED FAT 0.0G)
PROTEIN 1.8G CARBOHYDRATE 7.3G
CHOLESTEROL 0MG SODIUM 172MG

# Parsley-Garlic Rolls

2 tablespoons reduced-calorie margarine, melted
2 cloves garlic, crushed
1 (16-ounce) loaf frozen bread dough, thawed
1 tablespoon chopped fresh parsley
Vegetable cooking spray

**Combine** margarine and garlic; set aside.

**Cut** bread dough crosswise into 6 even portions with kitchen shears; cut portions in half crosswise.

**Roll** each half to ¼-inch thickness on a lightly floured surface; brush with margarine mixture, and sprinkle with parsley.

**Roll** each piece of dough, jellyroll fashion; place, swirled side down, in muffin pans coated with cooking spray. Cover and let rise in a warm place (85°), free from drafts, 1 hour or until doubled in bulk.

**Bake** at 400° for 10 to 12 minutes. Serve immediately. **Yield: 1 dozen.**

PER ROLL: 98 CALORIES (22% FROM FAT)
FAT 2.4G (SATURATED FAT 0.5G)
PROTEIN 3.0G CARBOHYDRATE 16.1G
CHOLESTEROL 0MG SODIUM 191MG

# Soup & Sandwich, Anytime

---

### Serves 4

Potato-Corn Chowder
Roasted Turkey-Pepper Sandwiches
Watermelon cubes (1 cup per serving)

*Total Calories per Serving: 602
(Calories from Fat: 10%)*

---

## Potato-Corn Chowder

¾ **cup chopped green pepper**
⅓ **cup chopped onion**
**Vegetable cooking spray**
2¾ **cups no-salt-added chicken broth**
1½ **cups finely chopped potato**
½ **teaspoon salt**
¼ **teaspoon pepper**
¼ **cup cornstarch**
2¼ **cups skim milk**
2¼ **cups frozen whole kernel corn**
1 **(2-ounce) jar chopped pimiento**

**Cook** green pepper and onion in a saucepan coated with cooking spray over medium heat, stirring constantly, 5 minutes or until tender.

**Stir** in chicken broth and next 3 ingredients. Bring to a boil; reduce heat, and simmer 5 to 7 minutes or until potato is tender.

**Combine** cornstarch and milk, stirring until smooth. Gradually add to potato mixture, stirring constantly.

**Stir** in corn and pimiento. Bring to a boil over medium heat, stirring constantly; cook, stirring constantly, 1 minute or until thickened. **Yield: 4 (1½-cup) servings.**

PER SERVING: 240 CALORIES (5% FROM FAT)
FAT 1.3G (SATURATED FAT 0.3G)
PROTEIN 9.7G CARBOHYDRATE 48.9G
CHOLESTEROL 3MG SODIUM 381MG

## Roasted Turkey-Pepper Sandwiches

2 **tablespoons fat-free cream cheese, softened**
1 **tablespoon reduced-fat mayonnaise**
1 **tablespoon spicy brown mustard**
⅛ **teaspoon pepper**
¼ **cup chopped commercial roasted red peppers, drained**
2 **tablespoons sliced green onions**
8 **slices pumpernickel bread**
¾ **pound sliced roasted turkey breast**
¼ **cup alfalfa sprouts**

**Combine** first 4 ingredients; stir in red peppers and green onions.

**Spread** mixture on one side of bread slices. Layer turkey and alfalfa sprouts on 4 slices of bread; top with remaining bread slices, and cut in half. **Yield: 4 sandwiches.**

PER SANDWICH: 310 CALORIES (14% FROM FAT)
FAT 4.8G (SATURATED FAT 1.1G)
PROTEIN 32.4G CARBOHYDRATE 34.4G
CHOLESTEROL 62MG SODIUM 530MG

Potato-Corn Chowder and Roasted Turkey-Pepper Sandwiches

# Patio Supper

## Fresh Corn and Crab Soup

2  cups fresh corn cut from cob (about 6 ears)
3¾  cups no-salt-added chicken broth
Vegetable cooking spray
1  tablespoon vegetable oil
1  cup chopped onion
3  cloves garlic, minced
3¾  cups 2% low-fat milk, divided
½  teaspoon freshly ground pepper
¼  teaspoon salt
½  teaspoon hot sauce
½  cup all-purpose flour
1  pound fresh lump crabmeat, drained

**Combine** corn and broth in a large saucepan. Bring to a boil over medium-high heat; stir occasionally. Reduce heat, and simmer 20 minutes.

**Coat** a skillet with cooking spray. Add oil; place over medium-high heat until hot. Add onion and garlic; cook, stirring constantly, until tender.

**Add** onion mixture, 3¼ cups milk, and next 3 ingredients to corn mixture; bring to a boil.

**Combine** flour and remaining ½ cup milk; stir until smooth. Add to corn mixture; cook over medium heat until thickened and bubbly, stirring often. Stir in crabmeat. **Yield: 6 (1½-cup) servings.**

PER SERVING: 320 CALORIES (22% FROM FAT)
FAT 7.7G (SATURATED FAT 2.6G)
PROTEIN 24.6G CARBOHYDRATE 38.4G
CHOLESTEROL 88MG SODIUM 404MG

## Healthy Slaw

4  cups finely shredded cabbage
2  cups finely shredded red cabbage
¾  cup shredded carrot
3  tablespoons sliced green onions
¼  cup low-fat mayonnaise
¼  cup plain low-fat yogurt
2  tablespoons white vinegar
1  teaspoon sugar
½  teaspoon pepper

**Combine** first 4 ingredients in a bowl; set aside.

**Combine** mayonnaise and next 4 ingredients; add to cabbage mixture, tossing well. Cover and chill. **Yield: 6 (1-cup) servings.**

PER SERVING: 61 CALORIES (44% FROM FAT)
FAT 3.0G (SATURATED FAT 0.5G)
PROTEIN 1.7G CARBOHYDRATE 7.9G
CHOLESTEROL 4MG SODIUM 98MG

## Peach-Blueberry Dessert

3½  cups peeled, sliced fresh peaches, divided
1½  cups fresh blueberries, divided
¼  cup unsweetened apple juice
⅛  to ¼ teaspoon ground nutmeg
3  cups vanilla low-fat ice cream

**Combine** 1 cup peaches, 1 cup blueberries, apple juice, and nutmeg in a saucepan. Bring to a boil, and cook 2 minutes, stirring occasionally. Remove from heat.

**Stir** in remaining 2½ cups peaches and ½ cup blueberries. Cover and chill. Spoon into individual dishes; top with ice cream. **Yield: 6 servings.**

PER SERVING: 159 CALORIES (18% FROM FAT)
FAT 3.1G (SATURATED FAT 1.8G)
PROTEIN 3.4G CARBOHYDRATE 32.2G
CHOLESTEROL 9MG SODIUM 58MG

# Garden Supper

Citrus Gazpacho
Shrimp Rémoulade Sandwiches
Summer Strawberry Dessert (¾ cup per serving)

*Total Calories per Serving: 407*
*(Calories from Fat: 15%)*

Citrus Gazpacho

# Citrus Gazpacho

1 large grapefruit
2 large oranges
1 cup chopped plum tomatoes
½ cup chopped green pepper
¼ cup peeled, chopped cucumber
¼ cup chopped tomatillo
2 tablespoons chopped purple onion
2 tablespoons chopped fresh cilantro
2 cloves garlic, minced
½ cup reduced-sodium vegetable juice
½ cup reduced-sodium tomato juice
¼ cup reduced-sodium fat-free chicken broth
2 tablespoons fresh lime juice
1 teaspoon hot sauce
Garnish: fresh cilantro sprigs

**Peel,** section, and seed grapefruit and oranges. Coarsely chop sections, and place in a bowl.

**Add** tomatoes and next 11 ingredients; cover and chill 4 hours. If desired, serve in coconut shells, and garnish. **Yield: 4 (1-cup) servings.**

PER SERVING: 99 CALORIES (6% FROM FAT)
FAT 0.7G (SATURATED FAT 0.0G)
PROTEIN 2.8G CARBOHYDRATE 23.2G
CHOLESTEROL 0MG SODIUM 24MG

# Shrimp Rémoulade Sandwiches

1½ cups coarsely chopped cooked shrimp
⅓ cup chopped celery
3 tablespoons nonfat mayonnaise
1 teaspoon chopped green onions
1 teaspoon capers
½ teaspoon tarragon vinegar
¼ teaspoon salt
¼ teaspoon prepared horseradish
4 (1-ounce) slices oatmeal bread, toasted
1½ cups shredded romaine lettuce

**Combine** first 4 ingredients in a small bowl, stirring well.

**Add** capers and next 3 ingredients, stirring well to combine.

**Place** bread slices on a serving platter. Divide lettuce evenly among bread slices. Spoon shrimp mixture evenly over lettuce. **Yield: 4 sandwiches.**

PER SANDWICH: 147 CALORIES (17% FROM FAT)
FAT 2.8G (SATURATED FAT 0.6G)
PROTEIN 13.5G CARBOHYDRATE 16.3G
CHOLESTEROL 92MG SODIUM 550MG

# Summer Strawberry Dessert

1 (1.3-ounce) envelope whipped topping mix
½ cup skim milk
1 teaspoon vanilla extract
2 (6-ounce) cartons strawberry low-fat yogurt
½ (10-ounce) commercial angel food cake, torn into bite-size pieces
2 cups fresh strawberries, sliced
3 kiwifruit, sliced
2 tablespoons sliced almonds, toasted

**Prepare** whipped topping mix according to package directions, using ½ cup skim milk and 1 teaspoon vanilla. Fold in yogurt, and set aside.

**Layer** half each of cake, yogurt mixture, strawberries, and kiwifruit in an 8-inch square dish. Repeat layers; sprinkle almonds on top.

**Cover** and chill at least 2 hours. **Yield: 8 (¾-cup) servings.**

PER SERVING: 161 CALORIES (19% FROM FAT)
FAT 3.4G (SATURATED FAT 1.7G)
PROTEIN 4.5G CARBOHYDRATE 28.4G
CHOLESTEROL 2MG SODIUM 128MG

# Sunday Night Special

## Vegetable-Beef Stew

1 pound lean beef tips, cut into ½-inch cubes
1 tablespoon vegetable oil
2 (10½-ounce) cans low-sodium, fat-free beef broth
4 carrots, scraped and sliced
4 medium onions, quartered
2 pounds red potatoes, peeled and cubed
2 (16-ounce) cans low-sodium whole tomatoes, undrained and chopped
1 (17-ounce) can whole kernel corn, drained
1 (16-ounce) can English peas, drained
1 (10-ounce) package frozen lima beans
1 tablespoon sugar
1 teaspoon garlic powder
½ teaspoon salt
½ teaspoon pepper

**Cook** beef in oil in a Dutch oven over medium heat, stirring constantly, until browned. Drain in a colander, and pat meat dry with paper towels. Wipe drippings from Dutch oven.

**Return** meat to Dutch oven. Stir in beef broth and remaining ingredients. Bring stew to a boil over high heat. Reduce heat, and simmer 1 hour, stirring occasionally. **Yield: 8 (2-cup) servings.**

PER SERVING: 362 CALORIES (12% FROM FAT)
FAT 4.8G (SATURATED FAT 1.2G)
PROTEIN 22.5G CARBOHYDRATE 59.1G
CHOLESTEROL 32MG SODIUM 419MG

## Honey-Banana Pops

2 (8-ounce) cartons vanilla low-fat yogurt
2 medium-size ripe bananas, peeled and mashed
2 tablespoons honey
1 teaspoon vanilla extract
¼ teaspoon ground cinnamon
8 (3-ounce) paper cups
8 wooden sticks

**Combine** first 5 ingredients in container of an electric blender or food processor; cover and process just until smooth.

**Pour** mixture evenly into paper cups. Cover tops of cups with aluminum foil, and insert a stick through foil into center of each cup. Freeze at least 4 hours.

**Remove** foil to serve, and peel paper away from each pop. **Yield: 8 pops.**

PER SERVING: 91 CALORIES (8% FROM FAT)
FAT 0.8G (SATURATED FAT 0.5G)
PROTEIN 3.1G CARBOHYDRATE 18.7G
CHOLESTEROL 3MG SODIUM 38MG

Vegetable-Beef Stew

# Casual Dining

Relax with this colorful assortment of carefree menus.
They'll take you from breakfast to lunch to dinner with few calories and
without a lot of fuss.

Grilled Flank Steak with Sweet Peppers, Roasted New Potatoes

Favorite Burgers, Dilled Garden Dip, Chicken with Ginger Sauce, Baked Catfish

Asparagus Salad, Quick Crouton Bread, Pear Snow with Berries, Cereal Medley

Gold Medal Chocolate Brownies, Whole Wheat Rotini with Pesto

Honey-Grilled Tenderloin (complete menu on page 58)

# Pretty Patio Party

(pictured on cover)

## Strawberry Spritzer

**2 (16-ounce) packages frozen unsweetened strawberries, thawed**
**1 (48-ounce) bottle white grape juice, chilled**
**2½ cups sparkling mineral water, chilled**

**Position** knife blade in food processor bowl, and add strawberries. Process until smooth.

**Combine** strawberry puree, white grape juice, and mineral water. Serve immediately in chilled glasses. **Yield: 8 (1½-cup) servings.**

PER SERVING: 152 CALORIES (0% FROM FAT)
FAT 0.1G (SATURATED FAT 0.0G)
PROTEIN 0.5G CARBOHYDRATE 39.2G
CHOLESTEROL 0MG SODIUM 24MG

## Grilled Flank Steak with Sweet Peppers

**2 (1-pound) flank steaks**
**2 tablespoons dry red wine**
**1 tablespoon low-sodium Worcestershire sauce**
**1 tablespoon red wine vinegar**
**1 tablespoon prepared horseradish**
**1 tablespoon tomato paste**
**½ teaspoon freshly ground pepper**
**2 teaspoons fresh thyme or ½ teaspoon dried thyme**
**2 cloves garlic, minced**
**1 sweet yellow pepper, halved and seeded**
**1 sweet red pepper, halved and seeded**
**1 sweet orange pepper, halved and seeded**

**Trim** all visible fat from steaks; score on both sides in 1½-inch squares, and place in a shallow dish or heavy-duty, zip-top plastic bag.

**Combine** red wine and next 7 ingredients; pour over steaks, and turn to coat. Cover or seal. Marinate steaks in refrigerator at least 8 hours, turning occasionally. Remove steaks from marinade, discarding marinade.

**Cook** steaks, covered with grill lid, over medium-hot coals (350° to 400°) 7 minutes on each side or to desired degree of doneness. Add peppers, cut side down, to grill during last 7 minutes of cooking.

**Chop** peppers. To serve, cut steaks diagonally across grain into thin slices. Top with chopped pepper. **Yield: 8 servings.**

PER SERVING: 230 CALORIES (51% FROM FAT)
FAT 13.1G (SATURATED FAT 5.5G)
PROTEIN 22.4G CARBOHYDRATE 4.9G
CHOLESTEROL 60MG SODIUM 78MG

# Roasted New Potatoes

24 small new potatoes (about 2⅔ pounds)
Olive oil-flavored vegetable cooking spray
¼ cup Italian-seasoned breadcrumbs
¼ cup freshly grated Parmesan cheese
¾ teaspoon paprika

**Cook** unpeeled potatoes in boiling water 15 minutes; drain and cool slightly. Quarter potatoes; coat cut sides with cooking spray.

**Combine** breadcrumbs, cheese, and paprika; dredge cut sides of potatoes in breadcrumb mixture.

**Arrange** in a single layer on a baking sheet coated with cooking spray. Bake at 450° for 15 minutes. **Yield: 8 servings.**

PER SERVING: 140 CALORIES (8% FROM FAT)
FAT 1.2G (SATURATED FAT 0.7G)
PROTEIN 5.1G CARBOHYDRATE 27.9G
CHOLESTEROL 2MG SODIUM 167MG

# Asparagus Salad

2 pounds fresh asparagus spears
½ cup lemon juice
¼ cup honey
2 tablespoons vegetable oil
Garnish: lemon curls

**Snap** off tough ends of asparagus. Remove scales from stalks, if desired. Arrange asparagus in a steamer basket; place over boiling water. Cover and steam 8 minutes. Plunge asparagus into ice water; drain and chill.

**Combine** lemon juice, honey, and vegetable oil in a jar; cover tightly, and shake well. Chill.

**Drizzle** lemon juice mixture over asparagus. Garnish, if desired. **Yield: 8 servings.**

PER SERVING: 80 CALORIES (39% FROM FAT)
FAT 3.5G (SATURATED FAT 0.6G)
PROTEIN 1.5G CARBOHYDRATE 12.8G
CHOLESTEROL 0MG SODIUM 2MG

# Quick Crouton Bread

½ (1-pound) loaf French bread
Butter-flavored vegetable cooking spray
½ teaspoon Italian herb blend
½ teaspoon garlic powder

**Slice** bread into 4 equal pieces; half each piece. Coat cut sides with cooking spray.

**Combine** Italian herb blend and garlic powder; sprinkle evenly over bread. Bake at 250° for 30 minutes. **Yield: 8 servings.**

PER SERVING: 84 CALORIES (8% FROM FAT)
FAT 0.7G (SATURATED FAT 0.2G)
PROTEIN 2.6G CARBOHYDRATE 15.9G
CHOLESTEROL 1MG SODIUM 165MG

# Pear Snow with Berries

2 (16-ounce) cans pear halves in juice, undrained
¼ cup evaporated skimmed milk
1 cup sliced fresh strawberries
1 cup fresh blueberries

**Drain** pears, reserving 1 cup juice. Cut pears into 1-inch cubes; place on an aluminum foil-lined baking sheet, and freeze 2 hours.

**Position** knife blade in food processor bowl; add pears. Process until chopped, stopping once to scrape down sides. Gradually add reserved juice and skimmed milk through food chute with processor running, processing until mixture is smooth.

**Pour** into a 9-inch square pan. Cover and freeze until firm, stirring every 30 minutes. Serve with berries. **Yield: 8 servings.**

PER SERVING: 73 CALORIES (4% FROM FAT)
FAT 0.3G (SATURATED FAT 0.0G)
PROTEIN 1.2G CARBOHYDRATE 17.7G
CHOLESTEROL 0MG SODIUM 14MG

# Summer Soiree

## Serves 8

Mimosas by the Pitcher
Green Goddess Dip (2 tablespoons per serving)
Skewered Beef and Chicken
Rice-Vegetable Pilaf
Sliced Tomatoes with Green Pepper Salsa
Dinner roll (1 per serving)
Frozen Fresh Peach Yogurt (½ cup per serving)

*Total Calories per Serving: 701*
*(Calories from Fat: 22%)*

## Mimosas by the Pitcher

1 (6-ounce) can frozen orange juice
    concentrate, thawed and undiluted
1½ cups club soda
2 (25.4-ounce) bottles champagne, chilled

**Combine** first 2 ingredients; add champagne. Serve over ice. **Yield: 8 (1-cup) servings.**

PER SERVING: 177 CALORIES (0% FROM FAT)
FAT 0.0G (SATURATED FAT 0.0G)
PROTEIN 1.1G CARBOHYDRATE 10.4G
CHOLESTEROL 0MG SODIUM 17MG

## Green Goddess Dip

1 (10-ounce) package frozen chopped spinach,
    thawed and well drained
½ cup trimmed watercress or fresh parsley
¼ cup coarsely chopped green onions
1 ripe avocado, peeled and halved
2 cloves garlic, sliced
¼ teaspoon salt
½ teaspoon hot sauce
1 (8-ounce) carton plain low-fat yogurt

**Position** knife blade in food processor bowl; add first 3 ingredients. Process 1 minute. Add avocado and next 3 ingredients; process until smooth. Add yogurt; process until blended.
**Chill.** Serve with vegetables. **Yield: 2¼ cups.**

PER TABLESPOON: 15 CALORIES (60% FROM FAT)
FAT 1.0G (SATURATED FAT 0.2G)
PROTEIN 0.7G CARBOHYDRATE 1.3G
CHOLESTEROL 0MG SODIUM 28MG

## Skewered Beef and Chicken

1 pound flank steak, partially frozen
1 pound skinned and boned chicken breast
    halves
¼ cup lime juice
1 tablespoon olive oil
2 cloves garlic, minced
½ teaspoon dried crushed red pepper
Vegetable cooking spray
Garnish: 4 limes, quartered

**Soak** 16 (12-inch) bamboo skewers in water.
**Trim** fat from steak; cut diagonally across grain into ¼-inch slices. Thread onto 8 skewers.
**Place** chicken between 2 sheets of heavy-duty plastic wrap; flatten to ¼-inch thickness, using a meat mallet or rolling pin. Cut into 1-inch-wide strips. Thread onto remaining skewers.
**Combine** lime juice and next 3 ingredients; reserve half of mixture, and chill. Brush remaining lime juice mixture on beef and chicken.
**Place** chicken skewers on a grill rack coated with cooking spray. Cook, covered with grill lid, over medium coals (300° to 350°) 5 minutes. Add steak skewers to grill rack; cook 10 minutes or until meat is done, turning skewers and basting meats with reserved lime juice mixture.
**Garnish,** if desired. **Yield: 8 servings.**

PER SERVING: 191 CALORIES (45% FROM FAT)
FAT 9.6G (SATURATED FAT 3.4G)
PROTEIN 23.7G CARBOHYDRATE 1.0G
CHOLESTEROL 65MG SODIUM 67MG

Skewered Beef and Chicken, Rice-Vegetable Pilaf, and Sliced Tomatoes
with Green Pepper Salsa

# Rice-Vegetable Pilaf

1⅓  cups water
1  teaspoon chicken-flavored bouillon granules
½  cup long-grain rice, uncooked
1½  cups sliced fresh mushrooms
1½  cups coarsely shredded carrot
½  cup chopped fresh parsley
⅓  cup thinly sliced green onions
¼  cup chopped sweet red pepper
¼  teaspoon pepper
¼  cup chopped pecans, toasted

**Combine** water and bouillon granules in a saucepan; bring to a boil. Add rice; cover, reduce heat, and simmer 20 minutes.

**Remove** from heat; uncover and stir in mushrooms and next 5 ingredients. Cover and let stand 5 minutes.

**Cook** over low heat 5 minutes or until excess moisture has evaporated. Sprinkle with pecans. **Yield: 8 (½-cup) servings.**

PER SERVING: 88 CALORIES (30% FROM FAT)
FAT 2.9G (SATURATED FAT 0.3G)
PROTEIN 2.0G CARBOHYDRATE 14.3G
CHOLESTEROL 0MG SODIUM 116MG

# Sliced Tomatoes with Green Pepper Salsa

1  cup chopped green pepper
¼  cup chopped green onions
1  tablespoon chopped fresh cilantro
2  teaspoons seeded, chopped jalapeño pepper
½  teaspoon ground cumin
¼  teaspoon salt
2  tablespoons cider vinegar
2  cloves garlic, minced
1  (4-ounce) container alfalfa sprouts
4  medium tomatoes, thinly sliced

**Combine** first 8 ingredients; cover pepper mixture, and chill 8 hours.

**Arrange** alfalfa sprouts on a serving plate; top with tomato slices. Using a slotted spoon, top with pepper mixture; drizzle with remaining pepper salsa liquid. **Yield: 8 servings.**

PER SERVING: 27 CALORIES (17% FROM FAT)
FAT 0.5G (SATURATED FAT 0.1G)
PROTEIN 1.5G CARBOHYDRATE 5.7G
CHOLESTEROL 0MG SODIUM 82MG

# Frozen Fresh Peach Yogurt

¼  cup sugar
2  cups mashed ripe peaches (about 4)
1  cup sugar
2  envelopes unflavored gelatin
Dash of salt
2  cups skim milk
5  cups plain low-fat yogurt
1  tablespoon vanilla extract

**Sprinkle** ¼ cup sugar over peaches; let stand 15 minutes.

**Combine** 1 cup sugar, gelatin, and salt in a saucepan; add milk, and let stand 1 minute. Cook over low heat, stirring constantly, 5 minutes or until gelatin and sugar dissolve; cool. Stir in yogurt, peaches, and vanilla; cover and chill.

**Pour** mixture into freezer can of a 1-gallon hand-turned or electric freezer; freeze according to manufacturer's instructions. Pack freezer with additional ice and rock salt, and let stand 1 hour before serving. **Yield: 25 (½-cup) servings.**

PER SERVING: 86 CALORIES (7% FROM FAT)
FAT 0.7G (SATURATED FAT 0.5G)
PROTEIN 3.7G CARBOHYDRATE 16.4G
CHOLESTEROL 3MG SODIUM 48MG

# Winning Menu

Cereal Medley (½ cup per serving)
Favorite Burgers
Dilled Garden Dip (2 tablespoons per serving)
Whole Wheat Rotini with Pesto
Gold Medal Chocolate Brownies

*Total Calories per Serving: 642*
*(Calories from Fat: 26%)*

## Cereal Medley

2  cups toasted oat O-shaped cereal
2  cups bite-size crispy wheat squares
2  cups bite-size crispy rice squares
2  cups pretzel sticks
1½  cups bite-size shredded whole wheat cereal biscuits
Butter-flavored vegetable cooking spray
1  teaspoon garlic powder
1  teaspoon ground celery seeds
½  teaspoon onion powder
1½  tablespoons low-sodium Worcestershire sauce
1  teaspoon hot sauce

**Combine** first 5 ingredients in a large roasting pan; spray thoroughly with cooking spray.

**Combine** garlic powder and next 4 ingredients; pour over cereal mixture, tossing to coat.

**Bake** at 250° for 2 hours, stirring and spraying with cooking spray every 15 minutes. Cool and store in airtight containers. **Yield: 18 (½-cup) servings.**

PER SERVING: 70 CALORIES (9% FROM FAT)
FAT 0.7G (SATURATED FAT 0.1G)
PROTEIN 1.8G CARBOHYDRATE 14.5G
CHOLESTEROL 0MG SODIUM 140MG

## Favorite Burgers

3½  cups shredded potato
2  pounds lean ground round
1  cup chopped fresh mushrooms
½  cup diced onion
½  teaspoon salt
½  teaspoon garlic powder
½  teaspoon pepper
½  teaspoon paprika
Vegetable cooking spray
16  hamburger buns

**Place** potato between paper towels, and squeeze to remove excess moisture. Combine potato, ground round, and next 6 ingredients. Shape into 16 patties.

**Coat** grill rack with cooking spray; place rack on grill over medium-hot coals (350° to 400°).

**Place** patties on rack, and cook, uncovered, 8 minutes on each side or to desired degree of doneness.

**Serve** patties in hamburger buns. **Yield: 16 servings.**

**Note:** To broil, place patties on rack coated with cooking spray; place rack in broiler pan. Broil 6 inches from heat (with electric oven door partially opened) 8 minutes on each side or until desired degree of doneness.

PER SERVING: 247 CALORIES (25% FROM FAT)
FAT 6.9G (SATURATED FAT 1.8G)
PROTEIN 15.9G CARBOHYDRATE 29.0G
CHOLESTEROL 48MG SODIUM 215MG

Whole Wheat Rotini with Pesto, Cereal Medley, and Gold Medal Chocolate Brownies

# Dilled Garden Dip

2  cups low-fat cottage cheese
2  tablespoons tarragon vinegar
1  to 2 tablespoons skim milk
1  tablespoon finely chopped green onions
1  tablespoon chopped fresh parsley
½  teaspoon dried dillweed
Dash of freshly ground pepper

**Combine** cottage cheese and vinegar in container of an electric blender; cover and process until smooth, stopping to scrape down sides as needed.

**Combine** cottage cheese mixture, milk, and remaining ingredients. Cover and chill 2 hours. Use as a dip with raw vegetables or as a condiment on hamburgers. **Yield: 2 cups.**

PER TABLESPOON: 11 CALORIES (8% FROM FAT)
FAT 0.1G (SATURATED FAT 0.1G)
PROTEIN 1.8G CARBOHYDRATE 0.5G
CHOLESTEROL 1MG SODIUM 58MG

# Whole Wheat Rotini with Pesto

3  tablespoons olive oil
1½  tablespoons water
½  teaspoon ground nutmeg
½  teaspoon salt
4  cloves garlic, minced
¾  cup chopped fresh basil
¾  cup chopped fresh parsley
1  cup grated Parmesan cheese
8  cups cooked whole wheat rotini (corkscrew pasta) or elbow macaroni (cooked without salt or fat)

**Combine** first 8 ingredients in container of an electric blender; cover and process 1 to 1½ minutes or until blended, stopping to scrape sides as needed.

**Combine** pasta and pesto mixture in a large bowl, and toss gently; serve pasta at room temperature. **Yield: 16 servings.**

**Note:** This dish may be prepared up to 1 day in advance. Prepare as directed, and chill.

PER SERVING: 143 CALORIES (28% FROM FAT)
FAT 4.5G (SATURATED FAT 1.4G)
PROTEIN 5.5G CARBOHYDRATE 19.7G
CHOLESTEROL 4MG SODIUM 169MG

# Gold Medal Chocolate Brownies

⅔  cup reduced-calorie margarine, softened
⅔  cup sugar
½  cup frozen egg substitute, thawed
3  tablespoons skim milk
1  teaspoon vanilla extract
⅔  cup all-purpose flour
½  teaspoon baking powder
¼  teaspoon salt
⅓  cup unsweetened cocoa
3  tablespoons finely chopped pecans
Vegetable cooking spray

**Beat** margarine at medium speed of an electric mixer until fluffy. Gradually add sugar, 1 tablespoon at a time, beating well. Add egg substitute, milk, and vanilla; mix well.

**Combine** flour and next 3 ingredients. Add to creamed mixture, mixing well. Stir in pecans. Spoon into an 8-inch square pan coated with cooking spray.

**Bake** at 325° for 30 minutes or until a wooden pick inserted in center comes out clean. Cool on a wire rack; cut into squares. **Yield: 16 brownies.**

PER BROWNIE: 113 CALORIES (49% FROM FAT)
FAT 6.1G (SATURATED FAT 0.9G)
PROTEIN 2.0G CARBOHYDRATE 13.4G
CHOLESTEROL 0MG SODIUM 124MG

# Sunset Supper

(pictured on page 49)

(pictured on page 49)

---

**Serves 6**

Honey-Grilled Tenderloin
Tomato-Cucumber Salad
Grilled yellow squash (½ cup per serving)
Breadsticks (2 per serving)
Easy Pineapple Sherbet

*Total Calories per Serving: 485*
*(Calories from Fat: 17%)*

---

## Honey-Grilled Tenderloin

2 (¾-pound) pork tenderloins
⅓ cup low-sodium soy sauce
½ teaspoon ground ginger
5 cloves garlic, halved
2 tablespoons brown sugar
3 tablespoons honey
2 teaspoons dark sesame oil
Vegetable cooking spray

**Trim** fat from tenderloins. Butterfly by making a lengthwise cut in each, cutting to within ¼ inch of other side. Place in a shallow container or large heavy-duty, zip-top plastic bag.

**Combine** soy sauce, ginger, and garlic; pour over tenderloins. Cover or seal, and chill at least 3 hours, turning occasionally. Remove tenderloins from marinade, discarding marinade.

**Combine** brown sugar, honey, and oil in a small saucepan; cook over low heat, stirring constantly, until sugar dissolves.

**Coat** grill rack with cooking spray; place rack on grill over medium-hot coals (350° to 400°). Place tenderloins on rack, and brush with honey mixture. (Keep basting sauce warm.)

**Cook** tenderloin 20 minutes or until a meat thermometer inserted in thickest portion registers 160°, turning once and basting frequently with honey mixture. **Yield: 6 servings.**

PER SERVING: 191 CALORIES (21% FROM FAT)
FAT 4.5G (SATURATED FAT 1.2G)
PROTEIN 24.2G CARBOHYDRATE 12.7G
CHOLESTEROL 74MG SODIUM 259MG

## Tomato-Cucumber Salad

¼ teaspoon salt
2 cups thinly sliced cucumber
¾ cup sliced green pepper
½ cup sliced fresh mushrooms
⅓ cup thinly sliced green onions
2 medium tomatoes, cut into wedges
3 tablespoons white wine vinegar
1 tablespoon olive oil
1 tablespoon water
1 clove garlic, minced
½ teaspoon dried basil
¼ teaspoon dried oregano
¼ teaspoon pepper
Leaf lettuce

**Sprinkle** salt over cucumber; toss gently, and let stand 30 minutes. Drain cucumber; press dry.

**Combine** cucumber, green pepper, and next 3 ingredients in a bowl; set aside.

**Combine** vinegar and next 6 ingredients in a small jar. Cover tightly, and shake vigorously. Drizzle over vegetables; toss gently.

**Cover** and chill 3 to 4 hours. Toss gently before serving, and arrange on lettuce leaves. **Yield: 6 (1-cup) servings.**

PER SERVING: 47 CALORIES (50% FROM FAT)
FAT 2.6G (SATURATED FAT 0.4G)
PROTEIN 1.4G CARBOHYDRATE 5.4G
CHOLESTEROL 0MG SODIUM 108MG

Easy Pineapple Sherbet

# Easy Pineapple Sherbet

**1 (15¼-ounce) can unsweetened crushed pineapple, undrained**
**1¼ cups unsweetened pineapple juice**
**¼ cup sugar**
**1 (12-ounce) can lemon-lime carbonated beverage, chilled**
**¾ cup evaporated skimmed milk**
**Garnishes: lemon and lime twists, mint sprigs**

**Drain** crushed pineapple, reserving ¾ cup juice; set pineapple aside.

**Combine** reserved juice, 1¼ cups pineapple juice, and sugar in a saucepan; bring mixture to a boil. Reduce heat, and simmer, stirring occasionally, 3 minutes or until sugar dissolves.

**Pour** into a large bowl; cover and chill. Stir in carbonated beverage and milk. Pour into freezer container of a 1-gallon hand-turned or electric freezer. Freeze according to manufacturer's instructions. Transfer to a large bowl; fold in crushed pineapple. Store in freezer. Garnish, if desired. **Yield: 6 (1-cup) servings.**

PER SERVING: 152 CALORIES (1% FROM FAT)
FAT 0.2G (SATURATED FAT 0.1G)
PROTEIN 2.9G CARBOHYDRATE 36.2G
CHOLESTEROL 1MG SODIUM 38MG

# Easy Cookout

## Grilled Vegetables

1 **medium onion, peeled**
4 **ears fresh corn, husked**
2 **medium-size red, yellow, or green peppers,**
  **seeded and halved**
1 **medium zucchini, quartered lengthwise**
1 **medium-size yellow squash, quartered**
  **lengthwise**
4 **large fresh mushrooms**
1½ **teaspoons salt-free lemon-and-herb blend**

**Place** onion in a steamer basket over boiling water; cover and steam 8 minutes. Remove from rack; cool slightly, and cut into 4 (¾-inch) slices. Set aside.

**Place** corn in steamer over boiling water. Cover and steam 8 minutes; remove from rack. Set aside.

**Place** pepper, zucchini, and yellow squash in steamer over boiling water. Cover and steam 3 minutes; add mushrooms, and steam 1 minute. Remove from rack; sprinkle with lemon-and-herb blend.

**Cook** vegetables, covered with grill lid, over medium-hot coals (350° to 400°) 8 minutes, turning once. **Yield: 4 servings.**

PER SERVING: 107 CALORIES (10% FROM FAT)
FAT 1.2G (SATURATED FAT 0.2G)
PROTEIN 3.8G CARBOHYDRATE 24.1G
CHOLESTEROL 0MG SODIUM 15MG

## Chicken with Ginger Sauce

2½ **tablespoons reduced-calorie orange**
  **marmalade**
⅛ **teaspoon grated lime rind**
1½ **tablespoons fresh lime juice**
½ **tablespoon grated fresh gingerroot**
4 **(4-ounce) skinned and boned chicken breast**
  **halves**

**Combine** first 4 ingredients. Place chicken on grill, and brush with half of marmalade mixture.

**Cook**, covered, over medium-hot coals (350° to 400°) 6 minutes. Turn and brush with remaining mixture; cook 6 to 8 minutes. **Yield: 4 servings.**

PER SERVING: 129 CALORIES (10% FROM FAT)
FAT 1.4G (SATURATED FAT 0.4G)
PROTEIN 26.3G CARBOHYDRATE 1.2G
CHOLESTEROL 66MG SODIUM 76MG

## Watermelon Sherbet

5 **cups seeded, cubed watermelon**
¾ **cup sugar**
1 **tablespoon lemon juice**
1 **envelope unflavored gelatin**
¼ **cup water**
1 **(12-ounce) can evaporated skimmed milk**

**Combine** first 3 ingredients. Cover; chill. Process in container of an electric blender until smooth.

**Sprinkle** gelatin over water in a saucepan; let stand 1 minute. Stir over medium heat until gelatin dissolves. Combine watermelon mixture, gelatin, and milk. Pour into freezer container of a 1-gallon freezer, and freeze according to manufacturer's instructions. **Yield: 9 (½-cup) servings.**

PER SERVING: 127 CALORIES (4% FROM FAT)
FAT 0.5G (SATURATED FAT 0.2G)
PROTEIN 4.2G CARBOHYDRATE 27.6G
CHOLESTEROL 2MG SODIUM 48MG

Grilled Vegetables and Chicken with Ginger Sauce

Baked Catfish, Asparagus Vinaigrette, and Cauliflower Sauté

# Jiffy Fish Bake

## Baked Catfish

**Baked Catfish**

¼ **cup yellow cornmeal**
¼ **cup all-purpose flour**
¼ **cup grated Parmesan cheese**
1 **teaspoon paprika**
½ **teaspoon salt**
½ **teaspoon ground black pepper**
⅛ **teaspoon ground red pepper**
1 **egg white**
2 **tablespoons skim milk**
4 **(4-ounce) catfish fillets**
**Butter-flavored cooking spray**
½ **teaspoon sesame seeds**
**Garnish: lemon wedges and strips**

**Combine** first 7 ingredients; set aside.

**Whisk** together egg white and milk. Dip fillets in milk mixture, and dredge in cornmeal mixture.

**Place** on a foil-lined baking sheet coated with cooking spray.

**Sprinkle** fillets with sesame seeds, and coat each fillet with cooking spray.

**Bake** at 350° for 30 minutes or until fish flakes easily when tested with a fork. Garnish, if desired. **Yield: 4 servings.**

PER SERVING: 196 CALORIES (27% FROM FAT)
FAT 5.9G (SATURATED FAT 1.9G)
PROTEIN 20.9G CARBOHYDRATE 13.4G
CHOLESTEROL 55MG SODIUM 460MG

# Asparagus Vinaigrette

1 **pound fresh asparagus spears**
2 **tablespoons rice vinegar**
1 **tablespoon water**
1 **tablespoon lemon juice**
1 **tablespoon olive oil**
¼ **teaspoon dry mustard**
¼ **teaspoon grated lemon rind**
⅛ **teaspoon ground white pepper**
4 **lettuce leaves**

**Snap** off tough ends of asparagus. Remove scales from stalk, if desired. Cook asparagus, covered, in a small amount of boiling water 6 minutes or until crisp-tender; drain.

**Plunge** asparagus into ice water to stop the cooking process; drain. Place asparagus in a shallow dish.

**Combine** vinegar and next 6 ingredients in a jar; cover tightly, and shake vigorously. Pour over asparagus; cover and chill. Serve on lettuce leaves. **Yield: 4 servings.**

PER SERVING: 49 CALORIES (66% FROM FAT)
FAT 3.6G (SATURATED FAT 0.5G)
PROTEIN 1.6G CARBOHYDRATE 3.8G
CHOLESTEROL 0MG SODIUM 3MG

# Cauliflower Sauté

2 **cups fresh cauliflower flowerets**
½ **cup sliced onion**
1 **clove garlic, minced**
1 **tablespoon olive oil**
1 **cup fresh or frozen snow peas**
1 **sweet red pepper, cut into strips**
½ **cup sliced fresh mushrooms**
1 **teaspoon dried oregano**
¼ **teaspoon salt**

**Arrange** cauliflower in a steamer basket; place over boiling water. Cover and steam 8 minutes; drain and set aside.

**Cook** onion and garlic in olive oil in a large nonstick skillet over medium heat, stirring constantly, until tender.

**Add** cauliflower, snow peas, and next 4 ingredients; cook, stirring constantly, until heated. **Yield: 4 (1-cup) servings.**

PER SERVING: 69 CALORIES (48% FROM FAT)
FAT 3.7G (SATURATED FAT 0.5G)
PROTEIN 2.3G CARBOHYDRATE 7.8G
CHOLESTEROL 0MG SODIUM 157MG

# Strawberries Marsala

1 **tablespoon plus 1 teaspoon Marsala wine**
2 **teaspoons sugar**
¼ **teaspoon lemon juice**
4 **cups fresh strawberries, capped**

**Combine** first 3 ingredients in a large bowl; add strawberries, and toss gently.

**Cover** and chill 8 hours. Toss before serving. **Yield: 4 (1-cup) servings.**

PER SERVING: 59 CALORIES (9% FROM FAT)
FAT 0.6G (SATURATED FAT 0.0G)
PROTEIN 0.9G CARBOHYDRATE 12.7G
CHOLESTEROL 0MG SODIUM 2MG

Shrimp Étouffée

# With Cajun Flair

## Shrimp Étouffée

——— **Serves 8** ———

Shrimp Étouffée
Mixed Green Salad
Bread Pudding with Whiskey Sauce

*Total Calories per Serving: 493*
*(Calories from Fat: 10%)*

2 pounds unpeeled medium-size fresh shrimp
3 cups water
Vegetable cooking spray
2 tablespoons reduced-calorie margarine
2 cups chopped onion
4 cloves garlic, minced
1 cup sliced green onions
3 tablespoons cornstarch
⅓ cup chopped fresh parsley
¾ teaspoon salt
¼ teaspoon ground white pepper
6 cups cooked long-grain rice (cooked without salt or fat)

**Peel** shrimp, reserving shells and tails; devein shrimp, if desired. Chop shrimp, and set aside.

**Place** shells and tails in a medium saucepan; add water, and bring to a boil. Cover, reduce heat, and simmer 30 minutes. Drain stock from shells, and set aside; discard shells and tails.

**Coat** a large, nonstick skillet with cooking spray; place over medium-high heat until hot. Add margarine, chopped onion, and garlic; sauté until tender.

**Add** 2 cups reserved stock; bring mixture to a boil. Add green onions and shrimp. Cook over low heat 5 to 7 minutes, stirring occasionally.

**Combine** cornstarch and ½ cup reserved stock; stir into shrimp mixture. Bring mixture to a boil; boil 1 minute, stirring constantly.

**Add** parsley, salt, and pepper; stir well. Serve over rice. **Yield: 8 servings.**

PER SERVING: 303 CALORIES (11% FROM FAT)
FAT 3.6G (SATURATED FAT 0.6G)
PROTEIN 21.2G CARBOHYDRATE 44.8G
CHOLESTEROL 129MG SODIUM 378MG

# Mixed Green Salad

3 cups torn romaine lettuce
3 cups torn Bibb lettuce
3 cups torn red leaf lettuce
3 cups torn endive
18 cherry tomatoes, halved
1 (8-ounce) bottle fat-free Italian dressing

**Combine** all ingredients, and toss gently. **Yield: 8 (1½-cup) servings.**

PER SERVING: 32 CALORIES (8% FROM FAT)
FAT 0.3G (SATURATED FAT 0.0G)
PROTEIN 1.4G CARBOHYDRATE 6.7G
CHOLESTEROL 0MG SODIUM 279MG

# Bread Pudding with Whiskey Sauce

⅓ cup firmly packed brown sugar
½ cup frozen egg substitute, thawed
2 cups skim milk
1 teaspoon ground nutmeg
1¼ teaspoons ground cinnamon
1½ teaspoons vanilla extract
5 cups (1-inch) French bread cubes
⅓ cup raisins
Butter-flavored vegetable cooking spray
Whiskey Sauce

**Combine** first 6 ingredients, beating with a wire whisk. Add bread and raisins; stir well.

**Spoon** mixture into eight 6-ounce custard cups coated with cooking spray.

**Place** cups in a large shallow pan; add hot water to pan to a depth of ¾ inch.

**Bake** at 350° for 25 minutes or until a knife inserted in center of pudding comes out clean. Spoon Whiskey Sauce over pudding. **Yield: 8 servings.**

## Whiskey Sauce

2 tablespoons sugar
1 tablespoon cornstarch
1 tablespoon reduced-calorie margarine
¾ cup water
¼ cup whiskey or bourbon

**Combine** all ingredients in a small saucepan. Cook over medium heat, stirring constantly, until mixture begins to boil; boil 1 minute, stirring constantly. Serve warm. **Yield: 1 cup.**

PER SERVING: 158 CALORIES (10% FROM FAT)
FAT 1.7G (SATURATED FAT 0.4G)
PROTEIN 5.2G CARBOHYDRATE 30.3G
CHOLESTEROL 2MG SODIUM 164MG

Grilled Polenta with Black Bean Salsa and Steamed Garden Vegetables

# Meatless Feast

## Serves 4

Grilled Polenta with Black Bean Salsa
Steamed Garden Vegetables
Spiced Peaches with Nutty Dumplings

*Total Calories per Serving: 608*
*(Calories from Fat: 9%)*

## Grilled Polenta with Black Bean Salsa

4  cups reduced-sodium, fat-free chicken broth
1  cup yellow cornmeal
**Vegetable cooking spray**
**Black Bean Salsa**

**Bring** chicken broth to a boil in a heavy saucepan; gradually add cornmeal, stirring constantly. Reduce heat, and cook 20 minutes or until mixture thickens, stirring often.

**Spread** cornmeal mixture into a 9-inch square pan coated with cooking spray; chill until firm.

Cut polenta into four squares; diagonally cut each square in half.

**Coat** a grill basket with cooking spray; arrange polenta triangles in basket. Cook, covered with grill lid, over hot coals (400° to 500°) 5 minutes on each side or until polenta begins to brown.

**Serve** with Black Bean Salsa. **Yield: 4 servings.**

## Black Bean Salsa

2  cups canned black beans, drained and
    rinsed
¾  cup finely chopped tomato
½  cup finely chopped onion
½  cup finely chopped sweet red pepper
¼  cup chopped fresh cilantro
1  teaspoon finely chopped jalapeño pepper
⅓  cup red wine vinegar

**Combine** all ingredients in a large bowl, and toss gently. Cover and chill. **Yield: 4 (1-cup) servings.**

PER SERVING: 296 CALORIES (6% FROM FAT)
FAT 1.9G (SATURATED FAT 0.2G)
PROTEIN 12.3G CARBOHYDRATE 55.9G
CHOLESTEROL 0MG SODIUM 263MG

## Steamed Garden Vegetables

½  pound carrots with tops, trimmed
½  pound broccoli flowerets
¼  pound zucchini, sliced
¼  pound yellow squash, sliced
¼  pound fresh mushrooms
1  medium-size sweet red pepper, cut into
    strips
1  medium-size green pepper, cut into strips
1  medium-size sweet yellow pepper, cut into
    strips
1  teaspoon dried Salad Supreme seasoning
Garnishes: lemon slices, fresh sage sprigs,
    parsley sprigs

**Arrange** carrots in a steamer basket, and place over boiling water. Cover and steam 8 minutes or until crisp-tender; remove and keep warm.

**Arrange** broccoli and next 6 ingredients in steamer basket over boiling water. Cover and steam 6 minutes or until crisp-tender.

**Arrange** vegetables on dinner plates; sprinkle evenly with seasoning. Garnish, if desired. **Yield: 4 servings.**

PER SERVING: 74 CALORIES (12% FROM FAT)
FAT 1.0G (SATURATED FAT 0.1G)
PROTEIN 4.1G CARBOHYDRATE 14.7G
CHOLESTEROL 0MG SODIUM 119MG

## Spiced Peaches with Nutty Dumplings

½  cup all-purpose flour
1  teaspoon baking powder
¼  teaspoon salt
¼  cup sugar, divided
2  tablespoons chopped pecans, toasted
¼  cup skim milk
⅛  teaspoon butter flavoring
2  cups sliced fresh peaches (about 1½
    pounds)
⅔  cup unsweetened white grape juice
¼  teaspoon apple pie spice

**Combine** flour, baking powder, salt, 2 tablespoons sugar, and pecans; stir well. Stir in milk and butter flavoring; set aside.

**Combine** peaches, grape juice, remaining 2 tablespoons sugar, and apple pie spice in a saucepan; stir well. Bring to a boil. Drop one-fourth of batter at a time into boiling peach mixture.

**Cover;** cook over medium heat 10 minutes or until dumplings are done. **Yield: 4 servings.**

PER SERVING: 238 CALORIES (11% FROM FAT)
FAT 2.9G (SATURATED FAT 0.3G)
PROTEIN 3.8G CARBOHYDRATE 52.2G
CHOLESTEROL 0MG SODIUM 157MG

# Wide-Eyed Brunch

## Whole Wheat-Oat Pancakes

⅔ **cup regular oats, uncooked**
½ **cup whole wheat flour**
½ **cup all-purpose flour**
1 **tablespoon baking powder**
¼ **teaspoon salt**
1 **cup skim milk**
¼ **cup frozen egg substitute, thawed**
2 **tablespoons vegetable oil**
**Vegetable cooking spray**

**Place** oats in container of an electric blender, and process until finely ground. Transfer to a large bowl, and add whole wheat flour and next 3 ingredients.

**Combine** milk, egg substitute, and oil; add to dry ingredients, stirring just until moistened.

**Coat** a griddle or nonstick skillet with cooking spray; place over medium heat until hot.

**Pour** ¼ cup batter onto hot griddle. Turn pancake when top is covered with bubbles and edges look cooked. Repeat procedure with remaining batter. Top each serving with 3 tablespoons Maple Syrup. **Yield: 4 (2-pancake) servings.**

PER SERVING: 252 CALORIES (30% FROM FAT)
FAT 8.4G (SATURATED FAT 1.5G)
PROTEIN 9.4G CARBOHYDRATE 36.1G
CHOLESTEROL 1MG SODIUM 203MG

## Maple Syrup

1 **cup firmly packed brown sugar**
½ **cup water**
¼ **teaspoon maple flavoring**

**Combine** sugar and water in a small saucepan; bring to a boil, stirring until sugar dissolves. Remove mixture from heat, and stir in flavoring. **Yield: 1¼ cups.**

PER TABLESPOON: 39 CALORIES (0% FROM FAT)
FAT 0.0G (SATURATED FAT 0.0G)
PROTEIN 0.0G CARBOHYDRATE 10.1G
CHOLESTEROL 0MG SODIUM 3MG

## Fresh Fruit with Lemon Yogurt

2 **oranges, peeled and sectioned**
1 **grapefruit, peeled and sectioned**
1 **banana, sliced**
1 **cup fresh or unsweetened frozen sliced**
   **strawberries**
2 **kiwifruit, peeled and sliced**
**Lemon Yogurt**
**Garnish: fresh mint sprigs**

**Combine** fruit, tossing gently. Serve with Lemon Yogurt, and garnish, if desired. **Yield: 4 servings.**

### Lemon Yogurt

½ **cup plain nonfat yogurt**
2 **teaspoons sugar**
1 **teaspoon lemon juice**

**Combine** all ingredients. **Yield: ½ cup.**

PER SERVING: 139 CALORIES (5% FROM FAT)
FAT 0.7G (SATURATED FAT 0.2G)
PROTEIN 3.7G CARBOHYDRATE 32.0G
CHOLESTEROL 1MG SODIUM 22MG

Whole Wheat-Oat Pancakes and Fresh Fruit with Lemon Yogurt

# Breakfast for Kids

—— Serves 8 ——

Breakfast Pizza
Sliced bananas (½ cup per serving)
Orange Frosty

*Total Calories per Serving: 374*
*(Calories from Fat: 26%)*

## Breakfast Pizza

¾ cup regular oats, uncooked
1 teaspoon sugar
¼ teaspoon salt
1 package dry yeast
1 tablespoon vegetable oil
½ cup warm water (120° to 130°)
⅓ cup whole wheat flour
⅓ cup all-purpose flour
Vegetable cooking spray
8 ounces Italian turkey sausage
1 cup (4 ounces) reduced-fat sharp Cheddar
    cheese
1 cup (4 ounces) part-skim mozzarella cheese
1½ cups frozen egg substitute, thawed
½ cup skim milk
¼ teaspoon dried oregano
⅛ to ¼ teaspoon freshly ground pepper

**Place** oats in container of an electric blender or food processor; cover and process until oats resemble flour.

**Combine** oat flour, sugar, salt, and yeast in a large bowl; add oil and water, mixing well. Add remaining flours; stir until blended.

**Turn** dough out onto a lightly floured surface; knead until smooth and elastic (about 5 minutes).

**Place** dough in a large bowl coated with cooking spray, turning to coat top. Cover and let rise in a warm place (85°), free from drafts, 1 hour or until doubled in bulk.

**Punch** dough down, and turn out onto a lightly floured surface. Roll dough to a 14-inch circle, and place on a 12-inch pizza pan coated with cooking spray. Turn dough under to form a ½-inch-high rim.

**Bake** at 425° for 15 minutes.

**Cook** sausage in a nonstick skillet over medium heat until browned, stirring to crumble. Drain; pat dry with paper towels. Spread sausage over crust; sprinkle with cheeses.

**Combine** egg substitute and next 3 ingredients; pour over sausage mixture.

**Bake** at 350° for 30 to 35 minutes. **Yield: 8 servings.**

PER SERVING: 234 CALORIES (40% FROM FAT)
FAT 10.3G (SATURATED FAT 4.3G)
PROTEIN 20.1G CARBOHYDRATE 15.4G
CHOLESTEROL 35MG SODIUM 472MG

## Orange Frosty

1 (6-ounce) can frozen orange juice
    concentrate, thawed and undiluted
1 cup water
1 cup skim milk
¼ cup sugar
1 teaspoon vanilla extract
Ice cubes

**Combine** first 5 ingredients in container of an electric blender; cover and process until mixture is smooth.

**Add** enough ice cubes to blender container to bring mixture to 6-cup level; blend until smooth. Serve immediately. **Yield: 8 (¾-cup) servings.**

PER SERVING: 71 CALORIES (1% FROM FAT)
FAT 0.1G (SATURATED FAT 0.0G)
PROTEIN 1.5G CARBOHYDRATE 15.9G
CHOLESTEROL 1MG SODIUM 17MG

# Company Fare

Whether it's an alfresco brunch or an elegant dinner party, healthy eating can fit your entertainment style. With these delicious light selections, guests won't notice that you've trimmed the calories and fat.

Steak Diane, Carrot-Sweet Potato Puree, Spinach-Kiwifruit Salad

Marinated Chicken Strips and Vegetables, Lemon Sherbet, Vegetable-Rice Toss

Poached Pears with Honey Sauce, Italian Beef Medaillons, Browned Rice Pilaf

Apple-Mushroom Pork Tenderloin, Chocolate Angel Food Cake

Herbed Cornish Hens (complete menu on page 88)

**Steak Diane and Carrot-Sweet Potato Puree**

# Celebration Dinner

## Serves 6

Steak Diane
Carrot-Sweet Potato Puree
Steamed broccoli (½ cup per serving)
French bread (1 slice per serving)
Poached Pears with Honey Sauce
Red wine (6 ounces per serving)

*Total Calories per Serving: 690*
*(Calories from Fat: 16%)*

## Steak Diane

6 (4-ounce) beef tenderloin steaks
1½ teaspoons salt-free lemon-pepper
    seasoning
**Butter-flavored cooking spray**
1 teaspoon margarine
2 tablespoons lemon juice
2 teaspoons Worcestershire sauce
1 teaspoon Dijon mustard
**Garnish: lemon twists**

**Sprinkle** steaks with lemon-pepper seasoning. Coat a large nonstick skillet with cooking spray; add margarine. Place over medium-high heat until margarine melts.

**Add** steaks to skillet, and cook 5 minutes on

each side or until desired degree of doneness. Transfer to a platter; keep warm.

**Add** lemon juice, Worcestershire sauce, and mustard to skillet; bring to a boil, stirring constantly. Pour over steaks. Garnish, if desired, and serve immediately. **Yield: 6 servings.**

PER SERVING: 180 CALORIES (42% FROM FAT)
FAT 8.3G (SATURATED FAT 3.1G)
PROTEIN 23.7G CARBOHYDRATE 1.1G
CHOLESTEROL 70MG SODIUM 110MG

## Carrot-Sweet Potato Puree

3  **cups thinly sliced carrot**
1  **(16-ounce) can cut sweet potatoes in light syrup, drained**
¼  **cup firmly packed brown sugar**
2  **tablespoons unsweetened orange juice**
½  **teaspoon ground cinnamon**
⅛  **teaspoon salt**
¼  **teaspoon vanilla extract**

**Cook** carrot in boiling water to cover 15 minutes or until very tender; drain. Position knife blade in food processor bowl; add carrot, sweet potatoes, and remaining ingredients. Process until smooth. Return mixture to saucepan to heat, if necessary. **Yield: 6 (½-cup) servings.**

PER SERVING: 113 CALORIES (2% FROM FAT)
FAT 0.2G (SATURATED FAT 0.0G)
PROTEIN 1.6G CARBOHYDRATE 27.0G
CHOLESTEROL 0MG SODIUM 108MG

## Poached Pears with Honey Sauce

1  **cup water**
1  **tablespoon lemon juice**
6  **medium ripe pears (3 pounds)**
6  **cups unsweetened apple juice**
**Honey Sauce**
3  **tablespoons chopped pecans, toasted**

Poached Pears with Honey Sauce

**Combine** water and lemon juice in a medium bowl; set aside. Peel pears, and remove core from bottom end, leaving stems intact. Dip in lemon juice mixture; set aside.

**Place** apple juice in a Dutch oven; bring to a boil, and cook over high heat until reduced to 1½ cups (about 12 minutes). Place pears, stem end up, in pan; cover, reduce heat, and simmer 12 minutes or until tender.

**Remove** pears with a slotted spoon, and cool slightly. Discard remaining apple juice. Cut pears lengthwise into 4 or 5 slices, leaving stem end intact.

**Spoon** 2 tablespoons Honey Sauce onto each dessert plate, and arrange pears on sauce. Sprinkle each with 1½ teaspoons pecans. **Yield: 6 servings.**

### Honey Sauce
½  **cup plus 1 tablespoon vanilla low-fat yogurt**
3  **tablespoons honey**

**Combine** yogurt and honey, stirring until blended. **Yield: ¾ cup.**

PER SERVING: 188 CALORIES (17% FROM FAT)
FAT 3.5G (SATURATED FAT 0.4G)
PROTEIN 2.0G CARBOHYDRATE 41.1G
CHOLESTEROL 1MG SODIUM 15MG

Spinach-Stuffed Tenderloin, Light Scalloped Potatoes, Orangy Carrot Strips, Chinese Cabbage Slaw, and Dinner Rolls

# Gourmet Buffet

─── Serves 16 ───

Hot Cranberry Cocktail
Spinach-Stuffed Tenderloin
Light Scalloped Potatoes
Orangy Carrot Strips
Chinese Cabbage Slaw
Dinner Rolls (1 per serving)
Raspberry sorbet (½ cup per serving)

*Total Calories per Serving: 637*
*(Calories from Fat: 23%)*

## Hot Cranberry Cocktail

1  **tablespoon whole cloves**
2  **teaspoons whole allspice**
1  **(32-ounce) bottle cranberry juice cocktail**
3  **cups unsweetened pineapple juice**
1  **cup water**

**Tie** cloves and allspice in a cheesecloth bag. Combine cranberry juice cocktail, pineapple juice, water, and spice bag in a Dutch oven; bring to a boil. Cover, reduce heat, and simmer 5 minutes.
**Discard** spice bag. **Yield: 16 (½-cup) servings.**

PER SERVING: 61 CALORIES (1% FROM FAT)
FAT 0.1G (SATURATED FAT 0.0G)
PROTEIN 0.2G CARBOHYDRATE 15.3G
CHOLESTEROL 0MG SODIUM 3MG

# Spinach-Stuffed Tenderloin

½ pound fresh spinach
Vegetable cooking spray
¼ pound fresh mushrooms, diced
¼ cup grated Parmesan cheese
¼ cup frozen egg substitute, thawed
½ teaspoon fennel seeds
½ teaspoon ground sage
½ teaspoon salt
½ teaspoon freshly ground pepper
1 (4½-pound) beef tenderloin, well trimmed
3 cloves garlic, crushed
¾ teaspoon fennel seeds
1 teaspoon freshly ground pepper

**Remove** stems from spinach, and wash leaves thoroughly. Drain. Place spinach in a nonstick skillet; cover and cook over medium heat just until spinach wilts, about 3 minutes, stirring once. Remove from heat; uncover and let cool.

**Chop** spinach; drain well, pressing spinach between layers of paper towels. Set aside.

**Coat** a nonstick skillet with cooking spray; place over medium-high heat until hot. Add mushrooms, and sauté until tender and liquid evaporates. Remove from heat; stir in spinach, Parmesan cheese, and next 5 ingredients.

**Trim** excess fat from beef tenderloin. Cut tenderloin lengthwise to within ½ inch of each end, leaving bottom of tenderloin intact.

**Combine** garlic, ¾ teaspoon fennel seeds, and 1 teaspoon pepper; rub over entire surface of tenderloin. Spoon spinach mixture into opening of tenderloin. Press gently to close. Tie tenderloin securely with heavy string at 1-inch intervals.

**Place** tenderloin on rack coated with cooking spray; place rack in a roasting pan. Insert meat thermometer into thickest portion of tenderloin.

**Place** tenderloin in a 500° oven; immediately reduce temperature to 350°. Cook 50 to 55 minutes or until meat thermometer registers 145° (medium-rare) or 160° (medium).

**Remove** tenderloin from oven. Cover loosely with aluminum foil, and let stand 10 minutes before slicing. **Yield: 16 servings.**

PER SERVING: 210 CALORIES (40% FROM FAT)
FAT 9.4G (SATURATED FAT 3.7G)
PROTEIN 28.6G CARBOHYDRATE 1.3G
CHOLESTEROL 81MG SODIUM 174MG

# Light Scalloped Potatoes

Vegetable cooking spray
2 cloves garlic, minced
⅓ cup diced onion
1½ tablespoons all-purpose flour
1 (12-ounce) can evaporated skimmed milk
1½ cups skim milk
1 teaspoon salt
½ teaspoon dried crushed red pepper
¼ teaspoon freshly ground black pepper
9 cups thinly sliced unpeeled red potato
   (about 4 pounds)
¾ cup (3 ounces) shredded Gruyêre cheese
⅓ cup freshly grated Parmesan cheese

**Coat** a Dutch oven with cooking spray; place over medium-high heat until hot. Add garlic and onion; sauté until tender.

**Add** flour; cook 1 minute, stirring constantly. Add evaporated milk and next 4 ingredients; cook over medium heat, stirring constantly, until mixture boils. Add potato, and return to a boil, stirring occasionally.

**Layer** half each of potato, Gruyére cheese, and Parmesan cheese in a 13- x 9- x 2-inch baking dish coated with cooking spray. Repeat layers.

**Bake** at 350° for 45 minutes or until bubbly and golden. Let stand 30 minutes before serving. **Yield: 16 (½-cup) servings.**

PER SERVING: 145 CALORIES (16% FROM FAT)
FAT 2.6G (SATURATED FAT 1.5G)
PROTEIN 7.5G CARBOHYDRATE 23.5G
CHOLESTEROL 9MG SODIUM 248MG

# Orangy Carrot Strips

8  cups thin carrot strips
2  teaspoons grated orange rind
¾  cup orange juice
2  tablespoons honey
1  tablespoon cornstarch
¼  cup water

**Combine** first 4 ingredients in a Dutch oven. Bring to a boil; cover, reduce heat, and simmer 8 to 10 minutes or until carrot strips are crisp-tender.

**Combine** cornstarch and water; stir into carrot strips, and bring to a boil, stirring constantly. Cook 1 minute, stirring constantly. **Yield: 16 (½-cup) servings.**

PER SERVING: 39 CALORIES (2% FAT)
FAT 0.1G (SATURATED FAT 0.0G)
PROTEIN 0.6G CARBOHYDRATE 9.5G
CHOLESTEROL 0MG SODIUM 20MG

# Chinese Cabbage Slaw

1  tablespoon sugar
⅓  cup cider vinegar
1  tablespoon sesame oil
10  cups shredded Chinese cabbage (about 2 pounds)
1  tablespoon sesame seeds, toasted

**Combine** first 3 ingredients in a small bowl; pour over cabbage, and toss gently. Cover and chill 8 hours.

**Toss** gently before serving, and sprinkle with sesame seeds. **Yield: 16 (½-cup) servings.**

PER SERVING: 44 CALORIES (51% FROM FAT)
FAT 2.5G (SATURATED FAT 0.4G)
PROTEIN 1.9G CARBOHYDRATE 4.9G
CHOLESTEROL 0MG SODIUM 74MG

# Dinner Rolls

1  package dry yeast
1½  cups warm water (105° to 115°)
2  tablespoons sugar
1  teaspoon salt
¼  cup plus 2 tablespoons reduced-calorie margarine, softened
4 to 4¼ cups all-purpose flour, divided
Vegetable cooking spray

**Dissolve** yeast in warm water in a large mixing bowl; let stand 5 minutes.

**Add** sugar, salt, margarine, and 1 cup flour; beat at medium speed of an electric mixer 2 minutes. Gradually stir in enough remaining flour to make a soft dough.

**Turn** dough out onto a lightly floured surface, and knead until smooth and elastic (about 10 minutes).

**Place** dough in a bowl coated with cooking spray, turning to grease top. Cover and let rise in a warm place (85°), free from drafts, one hour or until doubled in bulk.

**Punch** dough down, and divide into thirds; shape each portion into 12 rolls. Place in three 8-inch round pans coated with cooking spray.

**Cover** and let rise in a warm place, free from drafts, 45 minutes or until doubled in bulk.

**Bake** at 375° for 25 to 30 minutes or until golden. **Yield: 3 dozen.**

PER ROLL: 67 CALORIES (19% FROM FAT)
FAT 1.4G (SATURATED FAT 0.2G)
PROTEIN 1.6G CARBOHYDRATE 12.0G
CHOLESTEROL 0MG SODIUM 84MG

Italian Beef Medaillons, Browned Rice Pilaf, Cauliflower-Snow Pea Medley, and Spinach-Kiwifruit Salad

# Candlelight Dinner

### Serves 2

Italian Beef Medaillons
Browned Rice Pilaf
Cauliflower-Snow Pea Medley
Spinach-Kiwifruit Salad
Tangy Cranberry Ice
Sparkling water

*Total Calories per Serving: 538*
*(Calories from Fat: 20%)*

# Italian Beef Medaillons

½ pound lean eye of round, cut into 4
    (¼-inch-thick) medaillons, well trimmed
1½ tablespoons all-purpose flour
1½ tablespoons grated Parmesan cheese
¼ teaspoon Italian seasoning
¼ teaspoon garlic powder
⅛ teaspoon pepper
Vegetable cooking spray
⅓ cup green pepper strips
2 green onions, cut into ½-inch slices
¼ cup dry white wine
¼ cup water
½ teaspoon beef-flavored bouillon granules
1 teaspoon lemon juice

**Place** meat between 2 sheets of heavy-duty plastic wrap, and flatten to ⅛-inch thickness, using a meat mallet or rolling pin; set aside.

**Combine** flour and next 4 ingredients; dredge meat in flour mixture.

**Coat** a large nonstick skillet with cooking spray; heat over medium-high heat until hot. Add meat; cook 2 minutes, uncovered, on each side or until lightly browned. Remove meat from skillet; set aside.

**Add** green pepper and green onions; sauté 1 minute.

**Combine** wine and next 3 ingredients; add to skillet, and bring to a boil over medium heat. Return meat to skillet. Cover, reduce heat, and simmer 10 to 15 minutes, turning once. Add water, 1 tablespoon at a time, to prevent sticking, if necessary. To serve, spoon vegetables over meat. **Yield: 2 servings.**

PER SERVING: 208 CALORIES (28% FROM FAT)
FAT 6.4G (SATURATED FAT 2.5G)
PROTEIN 28.6G CARBOHYDRATE 7.4G
CHOLESTEROL 68MG SODIUM 371MG

# Browned Rice Pilaf

Vegetable cooking spray
¼ cup long-grain rice, uncooked
1 small clove garlic, minced
⅛ teaspoon dried oregano
⅛ teaspoon dried thyme
⅛ teaspoon salt
¾ cup water
2 tablespoons diced carrot
2 tablespoons diced sweet red pepper

**Coat** a medium saucepan with cooking spray; place over medium-high heat until hot. Add rice and garlic; sauté 3 minutes or until rice is lightly browned, stirring often.

**Add** oregano, thyme, salt, and water, stirring well. Cover, reduce heat, and simmer 15 minutes.

**Add** carrot and red pepper; toss gently. Cover and cook 5 additional minutes or until liquid is absorbed and rice is tender. **Yield: 2 servings.**

PER SERVING: 96 CALORIES (7% FROM FAT)
FAT 0.7G (SATURATED FAT 0.1G)
PROTEIN 1.9G CARBOHYDRATE 20.3G
CHOLESTEROL 0MG SODIUM 151MG

## Pilaf or Pilau

Pilaf, a rice-based dish also called pilau, originated in the Near East. You begin this classic dish by browning rice and then simmering it with a choice of vegetables, meat, poultry, or seafood. Depending on its ingredients, pilaf may be served as a main dish or side dish.

## Cauliflower-Snow Pea Medley

½ teaspoon chicken-flavored bouillon granules
¼ teaspoon dried basil
⅓ cup water
1 cup cauliflower flowerets
¼ pound fresh snow pea pods (about 34), trimmed

**Combine** first 3 ingredients in a medium saucepan; bring to a boil over medium heat. Add cauliflower; cover and cook 5 minutes.

**Add** snow peas; cover and cook 5 additional minutes. **Yield: 2 servings.**

PER SERVING: 39 CALORIES (12% FROM FAT)
FAT 0.5G (SATURATED FAT 0.3G)
PROTEIN 2.7G CARBOHYDRATE 7.1G
CHOLESTEROL 0MG SODIUM 222MG

## Spinach-Kiwifruit Salad

8 spinach leaves
8 Boston lettuce leaves
1 kiwifruit, peeled and sliced
Sweet-and-Sour Dressing
Garnish: lemon rind curls

**Arrange** salad greens on a platter. Top with kiwifruit. Serve with Sweet-and-Sour Dressing. Garnish, if desired. **Yield: 2 servings.**

### Sweet-and-Sour Dressing
2 teaspoons honey
1 teaspoon prepared mustard
⅛ teaspoon onion powder
½ teaspoon lemon juice
3 tablespoons water
2 tablespoons rice vinegar
1½ teaspoons vegetable oil

**Combine** all ingredients in a jar. Cover tightly, and shake vigorously. Cover and chill dressing. **Yield: ⅓ cup.**

PER SERVING: 92 CALORIES (39% FROM FAT)
FAT 4.0G (SATURATED FAT 0.7G)
PROTEIN 1.9G CARBOHYDRATE 12.8G
CHOLESTEROL 0MG SODIUM 54MG

## Tangy Cranberry Ice

1 cup cranberry juice cocktail
½ teaspoon grated orange rind
½ cup unsweetened orange juice
Garnish: thin orange slices

**Combine** first 3 ingredients; stir well, and pour into a freezer tray. Freeze until firm. Spoon frozen mixture into a small mixing bowl; beat at low speed of an electric mixer until smooth.

**Spoon** into chilled individual freezer-proof compotes; freeze until ready to serve. Garnish, if desired. **Yield: 2 servings.**

PER SERVING: 103 CALORIES (1% FROM FAT)
FAT 0.1G (SATURATED FAT 0.0G)
PROTEIN 0.5G CARBOHYDRATE 26.1G
CHOLESTEROL 0MG SODIUM 6MG

Tangy Cranberry Ice

# Pork with Pizzazz

## Apple-Mushroom Pork Tenderloin

2 (¾-pound) boneless pork tenderloins,
    trimmed
¾ cup all-purpose flour
½ teaspoon salt
¼ teaspoon pepper
Vegetable cooking spray
1 clove garlic, minced
1 cup sliced fresh mushrooms
¾ cup frozen apple juice concentrate, thawed
    and undiluted

**Cut** each tenderloin crosswise into 6 medaillons. Place medaillons, cut side down, between 2 sheets of heavy-duty plastic wrap; flatten to ¼-inch thickness, using a meat mallet or rolling pin.

**Combine** flour, salt, and pepper; dredge pork slices in flour mixture.

**Coat** a large nonstick skillet with cooking spray; place skillet over medium heat until hot.

**Arrange** pork in skillet, and cook until browned on both sides.

**Remove** pork from pan; set aside. Add garlic and mushrooms; cook 30 seconds, stirring constantly. Add apple juice concentrate and pork; simmer 3 minutes or until heated. **Yield: 6 servings.**

**Note:** Six 4-ounce skinned and boned chicken breast halves may be substituted for pork tenderloins.

PER SERVING: 275 CALORIES (14% FROM FAT)
FAT 4.2G (SATURATED FAT 1.4G)
PROTEIN 25.7G CARBOHYDRATE 32.5G
CHOLESTEROL 74MG SODIUM 253MG

Apple-Mushroom Pork Tenderloin and
Lemon Broccoli

# Lemon Broccoli

2 tablespoons grated lemon rind
¼ teaspoon salt
¼ teaspoon freshly ground pepper
1½ pounds fresh broccoli
2 tablespoons lemon juice

**Combine** first 3 ingredients; set lemon rind mixture aside.

**Remove** broccoli leaves, and cut off tough ends of stalks; discard. Wash broccoli thoroughly, and cut into spears.

**Arrange** broccoli in a steamer basket over boiling water. Cover and steam 5 minutes or until crisp-tender.

**Arrange** broccoli on a serving platter. Sprinkle with lemon rind mixture and lemon juice. **Yield: 6 servings.**

PER SERVING: 33 CALORIES (11% FROM FAT)
FAT 0.4G (SATURATED FAT 0G)
PROTEIN 3.4G CARBOHYDRATE 6.7G
CHOLESTEROL 0MG SODIUM 128MG

# Peach Melba Meringues

2 egg whites
¼ teaspoon cream of tartar
½ cup sugar
Melba Sauce
1 (16-ounce) can peach halves in light syrup, drained
1 tablespoon sliced almonds, toasted

**Beat** egg whites in a small bowl at high speed of an electric mixer until foamy. Add cream of tartar, and beat until soft peaks form. Gradually add sugar, 1 tablespoon at a time, beating until stiff peaks form.

**Spoon** meringue mixture into 6 mounds on a baking sheet lined with parchment paper. Shape mixture into circles, using the back of a spoon, mounding the sides at least ½ inch higher than the center.

**Bake** at 225° for 45 minutes. Turn oven off, and let meringues cool at least 1 hour before opening oven door. Carefully remove meringue shells from paper, and cool completely on wire racks.

**Spoon** Melba Sauce evenly into meringue shells. Top each with a peach half, cut side down, and toasted almonds. **Yield: 6 servings.**

## Melba Sauce

2 cups frozen raspberries, thawed
1 tablespoon Chambord or other raspberry-flavored liqueur
2 tablespoons powdered sugar
2 teaspoons cornstarch

**Mash** and strain raspberries. Combine raspberries, raspberry-flavored liqueur, powdered sugar, and cornstarch in a small saucepan. Cook over medium heat, stirring constantly, until mixture comes to a boil; cook 1 minute. Cool completely. **Yield: ¾ cup plus 1 tablespoon.**

PER SERVING: 148 CALORIES (5% FROM FAT)
FAT 0.8G (SATURATED FAT 0.1G)
PROTEIN 1.9G CARBOHYDRATE 35.3G
CHOLESTEROL 0MG SODIUM 21MG

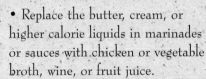

## Low-Fat Cooking Tips

• Replace the butter, cream, or higher calorie liquids in marinades or sauces with chicken or vegetable broth, wine, or fruit juice.
• Use dry-heat cooking methods (grilling, roasting, and skillet searing) to brown foods quickly while also locking in flavor and moisture.

# A Taste of the Orient

## Chinese Roast Pork

4 (8-ounce) pork tenderloins
¼ cup low-sodium soy sauce
¼ cup bourbon
1 clove garlic, minced
1½ tablespoons peeled, minced gingerroot
1 tablespoon sugar
Vegetable cooking spray

**Trim** fat from tenderloins; place in a shallow dish. Combine soy sauce and next 4 ingredients; pour marinade over tenderloins, turning to coat all sides. Cover and chill 2 to 3 hours, turning tenderloins occasionally.

**Remove** tenderloins from marinade, reserving marinade for basting. Bring marinade to a full rolling boil, and boil at least 1 minute.

**Place** tenderloins on a rack coated with cooking spray. Place in broiler pan; add water to pan.

**Broil** 6 inches from heat (with electric oven door partially opened) 15 to 18 minutes, turning often, and basting with reserved marinade. Meat is done when meat thermometer inserted in thickest portion registers 160°. **Yield: 8 servings.**

PER SERVING: 162 CALORIES (24% FROM FAT)
FAT 4.4G (SATURATED FAT 1.5G)
PROTEIN 26.2G CARBOHYDRATE 2.8G
CHOLESTEROL 83MG SODIUM 303MG

## Vegetable-Rice Toss

1 teaspoon sesame oil
¾ cup diced onion
½ cup diced carrot
2 cloves garlic, minced
2 (10½-ounce) cans low-sodium chicken broth
¼ teaspoon Chinese five-spice powder
¼ teaspoon pepper
¼ teaspoon salt
1¼ cups long-grain rice, uncooked
½ cup frozen English peas, thawed
½ cup diagonally sliced green onions

**Heat** oil in a wok or large nonstick skillet until hot. Add onion, carrot, and garlic; sauté until tender.

**Add** chicken broth and next 3 ingredients; bring to a boil. Stir in rice; return to a boil.

**Cover,** reduce heat, and cook 20 minutes. Add peas and green onions; toss gently. **Yield: 8 (⅔-cup servings.**

PER SERVING: 141 CALORIES (8% FROM FAT)
FAT 1.3G (SATURATED FAT 0.3G)
PROTEIN 3.8G CARBOHYDRATE 28.2G
CHOLESTEROL 0MG SODIUM 112MG

Chinese Roast Pork, Vegetable-Rice Toss, and Red Cabbage and Apple Slaw

# Red Cabbage and Apple Slaw

7 cups finely shredded red cabbage
1½ cups diced Golden Delicious apple
⅓ cup cider vinegar
2 teaspoons olive oil
1 teaspoon sugar
1 teaspoon Dijon mustard
¼ teaspoon salt
¼ teaspoon pepper
½ teaspoon caraway seeds (optional)
8 red cabbage leaves (optional)

**Combine** cabbage and apple, and set mixture aside.

**Combine** vinegar and next 5 ingredients in a jar; add caraway seeds, if desired. Cover tightly, and shake vigorously.

**Drizzle** over shredded cabbage; toss gently. Cover and chill thoroughly.

**Serve** slaw on red cabbage leaves, if desired.

**Yield: 8 (¾-cup) servings.**

Per Serving: 43 Calories (29% from Fat)
Fat 1.4g (Saturated Fat 0.2g)
Protein 0.9g Carbohydrate 8.0g
Cholesterol 0mg Sodium 99mg

# Lemon Sherbet

1 envelope unflavored gelatin
½ cup skim milk
¼ cup sugar
2½ cups skim milk
1 (6-ounce) can frozen lemonade concentrate, thawed and undiluted
½ teaspoon grated lemon rind

**Sprinkle** gelatin over ½ cup skim milk in a medium saucepan; let stand 1 minute. Add sugar, and cook over low heat until gelatin dissolves, stirring constantly. Remove from heat.

**Stir** in 2½ cups milk, lemonade concentrate, and lemon rind (mixture will curdle). Pour into an 8-inch square pan; freeze 3 hours or until mixture is firm but not frozen.

**Position** knife blade in food processor bowl; chop sherbet mixture into chunks, and place in processor bowl. Process until smooth.

**Return** mixture to pan; freeze 4 hours or until frozen. Let stand 10 minutes before serving.

**Yield: 8 (½-cup) servings.**

Per Serving: 98 Calories (2% from Fat)
Fat 0.2g (Saturated Fat 0.1g)
Protein 4.0g Carbohydrate 20.7g
Cholesterol 2mg Sodium 50mg

## Oriental Flavor Accents

• **Chinese five-spice powder** is a blend of equal parts of cinnamon, cloves, fennel seed, star anise, and Szechwan peppercorns. It has a pungent, slightly sweet licorice flavor and is used in Oriental cuisine.

• **Sesame oil**, a golden-brown seasoning oil pressed from toasted sesame seeds, adds an aromatic, nutty flavor. Two types are available—the darker version has a much stronger flavor.

• **Gingerroot** with its tan skin and pale yellow flesh offers pungent, spicy-hot flavor. To store, wrap unpeeled gingerroot in plastic wrap and place in a heavy-duty, zip-top plastic bag. Refrigerate up to 1 week, or freeze up to 2 months. To use, slice off a piece of the unthawed root; peel it, and then grate, mince, or slice.

• **Rice vinegar**, made from either fermented rice or rice wine, has a mild, slightly sweet flavor. Store at room temperature up to 6 months.

Marinated Chicken Strips and Vegetables, Whole Wheat Rolls, and Bellini Spritzers

# Lunch for the Ladies

## Quick Fruit Dip

1⅓  **cups plain low-fat yogurt**
¼  **cup low-sugar orange marmalade**
¼  **teaspoon ground cinnamon**

**Combine** all ingredients; cover and chill.
Serve with assorted fresh fruit. **Yield: 1½ cups.**

PER TABLESPOON: 9 CALORIES (20% FROM FAT)
FAT 0.2G (SATURATED FAT 0.1G)
PROTEIN 0.7G CARBOHYDRATE 1.1G
CHOLESTEROL 1MG SODIUM 9MG

# Bellini Spritzers

**6** ripe peaches (2 pounds)
**1** (750-milliliter) bottle champagne, chilled
**1** (23-ounce) bottle sparkling mineral water, chilled

**Peel** and halve peaches. Place in container of an electric blender or food processor; cover and process until smooth.

**Combine** 3 cups peach puree, champagne, and mineral water in a large pitcher. Pour into chilled wine glasses; serve immediately. **Yield: 12 (¾-cup) servings.**

PER SERVING: 80 CALORIES (1% FROM FAT)
FAT 0.1G (SATURATED FAT 0.0G)
PROTEIN 0.7G CARBOHYDRATE 9.1G
CHOLESTEROL 0MG SODIUM 14MG

# Marinated Chicken Strips and Vegetables

**¾** cup low-sodium soy sauce
**⅔** cup honey
**⅓** cup sherry
**½** teaspoon garlic powder
**¼** teaspoon ground ginger
**12** (4-ounce) skinned and boned chicken breast halves, cut into ¼-inch strips
**3** pounds fresh asparagus spears
**¼** cup coarse-grain mustard
**¼** cup sesame seeds
**7** cups torn Bibb lettuce
**7** cups torn romaine lettuce
**4** cups torn iceberg lettuce
**6** tomatoes, cut into 6 wedges each
**Honey-Mustard Dressing**

**Combine** first 5 ingredients in a 13- x 9- x 2-inch baking dish. Add chicken; cover and chill at least 2 hours.

**Snap** off tough ends of asparagus. Remove scales from stalks with a knife, if desired.

**Arrange** asparagus in a steamer basket over boiling water. Cover and steam 8 to 12 minutes or until asparagus is crisp-tender; drain. Cover and chill 1 hour.

**Drain** chicken, reserving ½ cup marinade; return chicken to baking dish. Bring reserved marinade to a full rolling boil, and boil at least 1 minute.

**Combine** coarse-grain mustard, sesame seeds, and reserved marinade; pour over chicken.

**Bake** at 350° for 30 minutes or until chicken is done, turning once. Remove chicken from marinade mixture, and drain on paper towels.

**Combine** lettuces; place 1½ cups on each of 12 serving plates. Arrange tomato, asparagus, and chicken evenly on lettuce. Serve with Honey-Mustard Dressing. **Yield: 12 servings.**

# Honey-Mustard Dressing

**¾** cup plain nonfat yogurt
**¼** cup reduced-calorie mayonnaise
**¼** cup honey
**2** tablespoons Dijon mustard
**2** tablespoons coarse-grain mustard
**1** tablespoon rice vinegar

**Combine** all ingredients in a small bowl; cover and chill. If desired, serve in individual scooped out lemon shells. **Yield: 1½ cups.**

PER SERVING: 262 CALORIES (20% FROM FAT)
FAT 5.7G (SATURATED FAT 0.9G)
PROTEIN 32.6G CARBOHYDRATE 22.0G
CHOLESTEROL 68MG SODIUM 484MG

# Whole Wheat Rolls

2 packages dry yeast
1¾ cups warm water (105° to 115°)
⅓ cup sugar
1 teaspoon salt
¼ cup vegetable oil
1 large egg, lightly beaten
2¼ cups whole wheat flour
2¼ to 2¾ cups all-purpose flour
Butter-flavored cooking spray

**Dissolve** yeast in warm water in a large mixing bowl; add sugar and next 4 ingredients. Beat at medium speed of an electric mixer 2 minutes. Gradually stir in enough all-purpose flour to make a soft dough.

**Turn** dough out onto a well-floured surface, and knead until smooth and elastic (about 5 minutes). Place in a bowl coated with cooking spray, turning to grease top.

**Cover** and let rise in a warm place (85°), free from drafts, 1 hour or until doubled in bulk.

**Punch** dough down; cover dough, and let rise in a warm place, free from drafts, until doubled in bulk.

**Punch** dough down, and divide in half; roll each portion into a 14- x 9-inch rectangle. Cut dough in half crosswise; cut each half into 9 (1-inch-wide) strips. Starting at short end, roll each strip jellyroll fashion into a spiral and place in muffin pans coated with cooking spray.

**Spray** tops of rolls with cooking spray. Let rise, uncovered, in a warm place, free from drafts, 40 minutes or until doubled in bulk.

**Bake** at 400° for 12 to 15 minutes; spray with cooking spray. **Yield: 3 dozen.**

PER ROLL: 81 CALORIES (22% FROM FAT)
FAT 2.0G (SATURATED FAT 0.4G)
PROTEIN 2.3G CARBOHYDRATE 14.1G
CHOLESTEROL 6MG SODIUM 68MG

Chocolate Angel Food Cake

# Chocolate Angel Food Cake

1 (14.5-ounce) package angel food cake mix
¼ cup unsweetened cocoa, sifted
¼ teaspoon chocolate flavoring
1 tablespoon sifted powdered sugar
Garnish: strawberry fans

**Combine** flour packet from cake mix and cocoa. Mix cake according to package directions; fold chocolate flavoring into batter. Spoon batter into a 10-inch tube pan.

**Bake** at 375° on lowest rack in oven 30 to 40 minutes or until cake springs back when lightly touched. Invert pan; cool 1 hour.

**Loosen** cake from sides of pan using a metal spatula; remove from pan. Cool on a wire rack.

**Sprinkle** cooled cake with sifted powdered sugar. Garnish, if desired. **Yield: 32 servings.**

PER SERVING: 52 CALORIES (2% FROM FAT)
FAT 0.1G (SATURATED FAT 0.1G)
PROTEIN 1.3G CARBOHYDRATE 11.5G
CHOLESTEROL 0MG SODIUM 95MG

# Easy Elegance

(pictured on page 71)

---
### Serves 8
---

Herbed Cornish Hens
Wild Rice and Mushrooms
Golden Carrots
Pears with Blue Cheese Dressing
Lemon Cake Pudding
Coffee

*Total Calories per Serving: 609*
*(Calories from Fat: 16%)*

## Herbed Cornish Hens

**4 (1-pound) Cornish hens, skinned**
**1½ cups light rosé**
**½ teaspoon garlic powder**
**½ teaspoon onion powder**
**½ teaspoon paprika**
**½ teaspoon poultry seasoning**
**½ teaspoon celery seeds**
**½ teaspoon dried basil**
**½ teaspoon pepper**
**½ cup light rosé**

**Remove** giblets from hens; reserve for other uses. Rinse hens with cold water, and pat dry. Split each hen lengthwise, using an electric knife. Place hens, breast side down, on a rack in a shallow roasting pan.

**Pour** 1½ cups wine over hens in pan. Combine seasonings; sprinkle half of seasoning mixture over hens. Cover and marinate in refrigerator 2 hours.

**Bake,** uncovered, at 350° for 1 hour. Remove from oven, and turn hens breast side up. Pour ½ cup wine over hens; sprinkle with remaining seasoning mixture.

**Bake** hens 30 additional minutes, basting every 10 minutes with wine mixture in pan. **Yield: 8 servings.**

PER SERVING: 159 CALORIES (35% FROM FAT)
FAT 6.1G (SATURATED FAT 1.7G)
PROTEIN 23.8G CARBOHYDRATE 1.0G
CHOLESTEROL 73MG SODIUM 73MG

## Wild Rice and Mushrooms

**3 cups canned no-salt-added chicken broth**
**¾ cup chopped onion**
**⅓ cup wild rice, uncooked**
**¾ cup long-grain rice, uncooked**
**1 (2½-ounce) can sliced mushrooms**
**1½ tablespoons chopped fresh parsley**

**Combine** broth and onion in a large saucepan; bring to a boil, and add wild rice. Cover, reduce heat, and simmer 20 minutes. Add long-grain rice and mushrooms; bring to a boil. Cover, reduce heat, and simmer 15 minutes or until liquid is absorbed. Sprinkle with parsley. **Yield: 8 servings.**

PER SERVING: 106 CALORIES (8% FROM FAT)
FAT 0.9G (SATURATED FAT 0.2G)
PROTEIN 3.3G CARBOHYDRATE 20.4G
CHOLESTEROL 0MG SODIUM 88MG

# Golden Carrots

4   cups thinly sliced carrot
1   cup unsweetened pineapple juice
1   cup water
2   teaspoons grated lemon rind
½   cup golden raisins
2   teaspoons reduced-calorie margarine
1   teaspoon vanilla extract
½   teaspoon ground mace

**Combine** first 4 ingredients in a saucepan; bring to a boil. Cover, reduce heat, and simmer 10 to 12 minutes or until tender.

**Remove** carrot mixture from heat, and drain, reserving ¼ cup liquid. Stir reserved liquid, raisins, and remaining ingredients into carrots. **Yield: 8 servings.**

PER SERVING: 64 CALORIES (11% FROM FAT)
FAT 0.8G (SATURATED FAT 0.1G)
PROTEIN 0.9G CARBOHYDRATE 14.5G
CHOLESTEROL 0MG SODIUM 30MG

# Pears with Blue Cheese Dressing

½   cup 1% low-fat cottage cheese
3   tablespoons skim milk
1   teaspoon Dijon mustard
½   teaspoon lime juice
¼   cup crumbled blue cheese
4   large fresh ripe pears
1   tablespoon lime juice
Romaine lettuce leaves (optional)
2   tablespoons chopped walnuts

**Combine** first 4 ingredients in container of an electric blender; cover and process until smooth. Transfer mixture to a bowl; stir in crumbled blue cheese. Cover and chill thoroughly.

**Slice** each pear in half lengthwise; remove core. Slice each half lengthwise into ¼-inch slices, leaving slices attached ½ inch from stem

end. Brush pear slices with 1 tablespoon lime juice.

**Arrange** romaine lettuce leaves on 8 individual salad plates, if desired. Arrange pear halves over lettuce, letting slices fan out slightly.

**Spoon** dressing evenly over pear halves, and sprinkle evenly with walnuts. Serve immediately. **Yield: 8 servings.**

PER SERVING: 87 CALORIES (28% FROM FAT)
FAT 2.7G (SATURATED FAT 0.9G)
PROTEIN 3.5G CARBOHYDRATE 13.7G
CHOLESTEROL 3MG SODIUM 128MG

# Lemon Cake Pudding

1⅓ cups sugar
⅓ cup all-purpose flour
1½ tablespoons grated lemon rind
⅓ cup lemon juice
½ cup frozen egg substitute, thawed
2 cups skim milk
6 egg whites
Vegetable cooking spray

**Combine** first 5 ingredients; gradually stir in milk. Beat egg whites at high speed of an electric mixer until stiff but not dry; fold egg whites into lemon mixture.

**Pour** into 8 (10-ounce) custard cups coated with cooking spray. Place cups in a large shallow pan; add hot water to pan to a depth of 1 inch.

**Bake** at 350° for 35 minutes or until edges are browned. **Yield: 8 (1-cup) servings.**

PER SERVING: 193 CALORIES (2% FROM FAT)
FAT 0.4G (SATURATED FAT 0.1)
PROTEIN 6.7G CARBOHYDRATE 41.7G
CHOLESTEROL 1MG SODIUM 94MG

# Brunch, Indoors or Out

## Serves 16

Spicy Pepper Soup
Crab and Marinated Potato Salad
Seasoned Toast Strips (4 strips per serving)
Citrus Punch
Raspberry Sauce with assorted fresh fruit
(2 tablespoons sauce per serving)

*Total Calories per Serving: 540*
*(Calories from Fat: 14%)*

## Spicy Pepper Soup

4 cups chopped sweet red pepper (1¾ pounds)
4 cups peeled and cubed potato (1½ pounds)
1½ cups chopped purple onion
4 cups water
2 (16-ounce) cans tomato sauce
1 cup dry, white vermouth
½ cup chopped fresh cilantro
¾ teaspoon ground cumin
¾ teaspoon ground red pepper
¼ teaspoon ground cinnamon
Garnish: fresh cilantro sprigs

**Combine** first 4 ingredients in a Dutch oven; bring to a boil. Cover, reduce heat, and simmer 20 minutes or until vegetables are tender.

**Stir** in tomato sauce and next 5 ingredients.

**Bring** to a boil; reduce heat, and simmer 10 minutes.

**Place** half of mixture in container of an electric blender; cover and process until smooth, stopping once to scrape down sides. Remove mixture, and repeat procedure. Garnish, if desired. **Yield: 16 (¾-cup) servings.**

PER SERVING: 88 CALORIES (4% FROM FAT)
FAT 0.4G (SATURATED FAT 0.1G)
PROTEIN 2.3G CARBOHYDRATE 16.7G
CHOLESTEROL 0MG SODIUM 351MG

## Crab and Marinated Potato Salad

3 pounds fresh lump crabmeat, drained
2 cups finely chopped celery
⅓ cup chopped green onions
¾ cup nonfat mayonnaise
1 (7-ounce) jar diced pimiento, drained
3 tablespoons lemon juice
½ teaspoon salt
¼ teaspoon garlic powder
¼ teaspoon ground red pepper
Red leaf lettuce
Marinated Potato Slices
1½ cups cucumber slices
2 cups tomato wedges

**Combine** first 9 ingredients. Serve on lettuce leaves with Marinated Potato Slices, cucumber slices, and tomato wedges. **Yield: 16 servings.**

### Marinated Potato Slices

8 red potatoes (1¼ pounds)
1 cup olive oil
⅓ cup red wine vinegar
2 tablespoons Dijon mustard
½ teaspoon salt
¼ teaspoon ground white pepper

**Cook** potatoes in boiling water to cover 8 minutes or just until tender. Cool and cut into thin slices; place in a large bowl. Set aside.

**Combine** olive oil and next 4 ingredients; pour over potato slices.

**Cover** and chill 8 hours. Drain before serving. **Yield: 4 cups.**

PER SERVING: 196 CALORIES (26% FROM FAT)
FAT 5.7G (SATURATED FAT 0.8G)
PROTEIN 19.4G CARBOHYDRATE 16.9G
CHOLESTEROL 85MG SODIUM 465MG

## Seasoned Toast Strips

**16 slices thin-sliced white bread**
**Butter-flavored cooking spray**
**1 tablespoon salad seasoning**

**Remove** crust from bread; coat one side of each slice with cooking spray. Lightly sprinkle coated side with salad seasoning, and cut into 4 strips.

**Place** strips on baking sheets; bake at 325° for 12 to15 minutes or until lightly browned. **Yield: 16 servings.**

PER SERVING: 73 CALORIES (16% FROM FAT)
FAT 1.3G (SATURATED FAT 0.2G)
PROTEIN 2.2G CARBOHYDRATE 12.6G
CHOLESTEROL 1MG SODIUM 181MG

## Citrus Punch

**1 cup water**
**¼ cup sugar**
**3 cups unsweetened pineapple juice**
**3 cups water**
**1 (6-ounce) can frozen orange juice**
**    concentrate, thawed and undiluted**
**½ cup lemon juice**
**3 (12-ounce) cans lemon-lime carbonated**
**    beverage, chilled**
**Garnish: lemon slices**

**Combine** 1 cup water and sugar in a small saucepan; cook over low heat, stirring constantly, until sugar dissolves. Remove from heat; cool.

**Combine** sugar mixture, pineapple juice, and next 3 ingredients in a 3-quart container; cover and chill. Just before serving, stir in carbonated beverage; serve over ice. Garnish, if desired. **Yield: 16 (¾-cup) servings.**

PER SERVING: 91 CALORIES (2% FROM FAT)
FAT 0.2G (SATURATED FAT 0.0G)
PROTEIN 0.2G CARBOHYDRATE 22.8G
CHOLESTEROL 0MG SODIUM 8MG

Raspberry Sauce with assorted fresh fruit

## Raspberry Sauce

**2 (10-ounce) packages frozen raspberries in**
**    light syrup, thawed**
**Garnish: fresh mint sprigs**

**Position** knife blade in food processor bowl; add raspberries. Process until smooth, stopping once to scrape down sides.

**Pour** through a wire-mesh strainer into a bowl, discarding seeds. Chill. Serve with fresh fruit. Garnish, if desired. **Yield: 2 cups.**

PER TABLESPOON: 18 CALORIES (0% FROM FAT)
FAT 0.0G (SATURATED FAT 0.0G)
PROTEIN 0.1G CARBOHYDRATE 4.6G
CHOLESTEROL 0MG SODIUM 0MG

Grilled Tuna with Poblano Salsa, Yellow Rice, and Summer Vegetables

# Alfresco Summer Supper

## Grilled Tuna with Poblano Salsa

2  tablespoons lime juice
1  teaspoon olive oil
4  (4-ounce) tuna steaks
Vegetable cooking spray
Poblano Salsa

**Combine** lime juice and olive oil; brush on tuna steaks. Coat grill rack with cooking spray; place on grill over medium-hot coals.

**Cook** tuna steaks, covered with grill lid, over medium-hot coals (350° to 400°) 5 minutes on each side or until done. Serve with Poblano Salsa. **Yield: 4 servings.**

### Poblano Salsa

4  medium-size poblano chiles
⅓  cup fresh or canned tomatillo
1  small serrano or jalapeño chile, seeded and diced
½  cup chopped tomato
¼  cup diced onion
2  tablespoons chopped fresh parsley or cilantro
2  tablespoons lime juice
½  teaspoon ground cumin
½  teaspoon salt

**Place** poblano chiles on a baking sheet; broil 6 inches from heat (with electric oven door partially opened), turning often with tongs until peppers are blistered on all sides. Immediately place in a heavy-duty, zip-top plastic bag; seal and let steam 10 to 15 minutes. Remove peel of each chile; seed and dice chiles.

**Combine** chiles, tomatillo, and remaining ingredients. Cover and chill. **Yield: 2 cups.**

**Note:** Two 4.5-ounce cans chopped green chiles may be substituted for poblano chiles.

PER SERVING: 185 CALORIES (34% FROM FAT)
FAT 7.0G (SATURATED FAT 1.6G)
PROTEIN 26.7G CARBOHYDRATE 2.3G
CHOLESTEROL 43MG SODIUM 133MG

## Yellow Rice

Olive oil-flavored vegetable cooking spray
¼  cup diced onion
2  cups no-salt-added chicken broth
1  cup long-grain rice, uncooked
¼  teaspoon salt
⅛  teaspoon ground turmeric
1  bay leaf

**Coat** a nonstick skillet with cooking spray; place over medium-high heat until hot. Add onion, and sauté until tender.

**Add** broth and remaining ingredients. Bring to a boil; cover, reduce heat, and simmer 20 minutes or until rice is tender and liquid is absorbed. Remove and discard bay leaf. **Yield: 4 (½-cup) servings**.

PER SERVING: 185 CALORIES (2% FROM FAT)
FAT 0.5G (SATURATED FAT 0.1G)
PROTEIN 3.7G CARBOHYDRATE 38.9G
CHOLESTEROL 0MG SODIUM 152MG

## Summer Vegetables

Vegetable cooking spray
4 cloves garlic, minced
2 cups sliced zucchini
2 cups sliced yellow squash
1 cup chopped tomato
½ cup julienne-sliced green pepper
½ cup ready-to-serve, no-salt-added chicken
   broth
1 tablespoon chopped fresh basil or
   1 teaspoon dried basil

**Coat** a large nonstick skillet with cooking spray; place over medium-high heat until hot. Add garlic, and cook 1 minute.

**Add** zucchini and next 4 ingredients. Cook 3 minutes or until vegetables are crisp-tender, stirring constantly. Stir in basil. **Yield: 4 (¾-cup) servings.**

PER SERVING: 44 CALORIES (14% FROM FAT)
FAT 0.7G (SATURATED FAT 0.1G)
PROTEIN 2.3G CARBOHYDRATE 8.7G
CHOLESTEROL 0MG SODIUM 9MG

### Low-Fat Cooking Tips

• Save fat calories by using vegetable cooking spray in place of margarine or oil to grease skillets and baking pans.
• Instead of serving sauces or cream over vegetables, use seasonings such as bouillon, herbs, spices, and lemon juice.

## Four-Flavor Pound Cake

Vegetable cooking spray
1¾ cups sifted cake flour
2 teaspoons baking powder
¼ teaspoon salt
¾ cup sugar
½ cup vegetable oil
½ cup skim milk
½ teaspoon grated lemon rind
¼ teaspoon almond extract
¼ teaspoon rum extract
¼ teaspoon lemon extract
¼ teaspoon vanilla extract
**4 egg whites, stiffly beaten**
**Fresh strawberries**

**Coat** the bottom of an 8½- x 4½- x 3-inch loafpan with cooking spray; dust with flour, and set aside.

**Combine** 1¾ cups cake flour and next 3 ingredients in a large bowl. Add oil and milk; beat at medium speed of an electric mixer until batter is smooth (batter will be thick).

**Add** lemon rind and next 4 ingredients; fold in about one-third of egg whites. Gently fold in remaining egg whites.

**Spoon** batter into pan. Bake at 350° for 40 minutes or until a wooden pick inserted in center comes out clean.

**Cool** in pan 10 minutes; remove from pan, and cool on a wire rack. Serve ¾ cup fresh strawberries with each slice. **Yield: 16 servings.**

PER SERVING: 182 CALORIES (37% FROM FAT)
FAT 7.4G (SATURATED FAT 1.3G)
PROTEIN 2.8G CARBOHYDRATE 27.1G
CHOLESTEROL 0MG SODIUM 55MG

# Holiday Celebrations

Welcome the holidays! These menus prove you can avoid the
rich party circuit and still treat your family and friends
to their favorite celebration foods.

Country Crab Cakes, Rosemary Roasted Potatoes, Anadama Rolls

Honey-Glazed Turkey Breast, Twice-Baked Potato, Light-Style Cranberry Relish

Strawberry-Champagne Sorbet, Beef Tenderloin for Two, Holiday Potatoes with Chives

Green Chile Quesadillas, Chicken Enchiladas, Jicama-Orange Salad

Apricot-Glazed Ham (complete menu on page 100)

# Toast the New Year

## Country Crab Cakes

3  ounces thinly sliced country ham, trimmed
¼  cup frozen egg substitute, thawed
1  tablespoon baking powder
1  teaspoon Old Bay seasoning
1  tablespoon chopped fresh parsley
1  tablespoon reduced-sodium Worcestershire
     sauce
1  tablespoon reduced-fat mayonnaise
2  slices white bread
1  pound fresh jumbo lump crabmeat, drained
Vegetable cooking spray
Lemon wedges

Country Crab Cakes and Rosemary Roasted Potatoes

**Place** ham in a large nonstick skillet, overlapping slices as needed. Add water to cover. Cook over high heat 3 minutes. Remove ham, and drain. Finely chop ham; set aside.

**Combine** egg substitute and next 5 ingredients in a large bowl; set aside.

**Remove** and discard crusts from bread. Tear bread into ½-inch pieces; add bread and ham to egg substitute mixture. Let stand until liquid is absorbed. Stir well. Fold in crabmeat, and shape into 8 patties.

**Cook** patties in a nonstick skillet coated with cooking spray until lightly browned, turning once. Serve with lemon wedges. **Yield: 4 (2-patty) servings.**

PER SERVING: 194 CALORIES (25% FROM FAT)
FAT 5.3G (SATURATED FAT 0.5G)
PROTEIN 26.4G CARBOHYDRATE 8.7G
CHOLESTEROL 99MG SODIUM 1103MG

# Rosemary Roasted Potatoes

3 large baking potatoes, unpeeled
Olive oil-flavored cooking spray
¼ teaspoon salt
1½ teaspoons fresh or dried rosemary
½ teaspoon freshly ground pepper
Garnish: fresh rosemary sprigs

**Wash** potatoes, and pat dry; cut into ¼-inch slices. Arrange slices into 4 rows on a baking sheet coated with cooking spray, overlapping half of each slice with the next. Sprinkle with salt.

**Combine** rosemary and pepper; sprinkle potato slices with half of mixture. Set remaining mixture aside.

**Bake** at 375° for 20 minutes; turn potato slices over. Coat potato slices with cooking spray, and sprinkle with remaining rosemary mixture. Bake 20 additional minutes. Garnish, if desired. **Yield: 4 servings.**

PER SERVING: 110 CALORIES (7% FROM FAT)
FAT 0.9G (SATURATED FAT 0.0G)
PROTEIN 3.1G CARBOHYDRATE 23.3G
CHOLESTEROL 0MG SODIUM 157MG

# Strawberry-Champagne Sorbet

½ cup sugar
½ cup water
1 (10-ounce) package frozen strawberries, thawed
2 tablespoons lemon juice
1½ cups champagne
12 fresh strawberries

**Combine** sugar and water in a heavy saucepan; cook over medium heat, stirring constantly, until sugar dissolves. Remove sugar syrup from heat; cool.

**Place** thawed strawberries in container of an electric blender or food processor; cover and process until strawberries are smooth. Pour mixture through a wire-mesh strainer into an 8-inch square pan, pressing with back of spoon against sides of strainer to squeeze out juice. Discard pulp and seeds.

**Stir** lemon juice, sugar syrup, and champagne into strawberry puree. Cover and freeze 4 hours.

**Position** knife blade in food processor bowl; add frozen mixture, and process until smooth. Return to pan, and freeze until firm. Repeat processing procedure, and return mixture to pan; freeze until firm.

**Spoon** into glasses, and serve with fresh strawberries. **Yield: 6 (½-cup) servings.**

PER SERVING: 136 CALORIES (1% FROM FAT)
FAT 0.2G (SATURATED FAT 0.0G)
PROTEIN 0.6G CARBOHYDRATE 24.2G
CHOLESTEROL 0MG SODIUM 4MG

# Be My Valentine

## Beef Tenderloin for Two

2 (4-ounce) beef tenderloin steaks
1 large clove garlic, crushed
¼ teaspoon cracked pepper
¾ cup canned no-salt-added beef broth
2 tablespoons Madeira wine
2 cups sliced fresh mushrooms
1 cup fresh whole green beans
2 small tomatoes, cut into wedges
Vegetable cooking spray

**Rub** both sides of steaks with garlic, and sprinkle with pepper; set aside.

**Combine** beef broth and wine in a medium skillet; bring to a boil over medium heat. Add mushrooms and green beans, keeping them separated in skillet.

**Cover**, reduce heat, and simmer 7 minutes or until beans are crisp-tender. Add tomato; heat thoroughly.

**Place** steaks on rack coated with cooking spray; place in broiler pan. Broil 6 inches from heat (with electric oven door partially opened) 5 minutes on each side or until meat thermometer registers 145° (medium-rare) or 160° (medium).

**Arrange** vegetables on serving plates, reserving liquid; place steak on mushrooms. Reduce reserved liquid over high heat to 1 tablespoon; drizzle over steaks. **Yield: 2 servings.**

PER SERVING: 244 CALORIES (33% FROM FAT)
FAT 8.9G (SATURATED FAT 3.2G)
PROTEIN 27.6G CARBOHYDRATE 13.4G
CHOLESTEROL 71MG SODIUM 72MG

## Twice-Baked Potato

1 (12-ounce) baking potato
3 tablespoons light process cream cheese
3 tablespoons plain nonfat yogurt
2 teaspoons chopped fresh chives or
    ¾ teaspoon freeze-dried chives
¼ teaspoon pepper
⅛ teaspoon salt
⅛ teaspoon paprika

**Wash** potato; prick several times with a fork. Place potato on a paper towel in microwave oven. Microwave at HIGH 4 to 6 minutes. Let potato stand 5 minutes.

**Cut** potato in half lengthwise; carefully scoop out pulp, leaving shells intact. Combine potato pulp, cream cheese, and next 4 ingredients.

**Stuff** shells with potato mixture; sprinkle evenly with paprika. Place on a microwave-safe plate; microwave at HIGH 1 minute or until hot. **Yield: 2 servings.**

PER SERVING: 244 CALORIES (14% FROM FAT)
FAT 3.8G (SATURATED FAT 2.2G)
PROTEIN 7.2G CARBOHYDRATE 46.1G
CHOLESTEROL 13MG SODIUM 295MG

Beef Tenderloin for Two and Twice-Baked Potato

# An Easter Tradition

(pictured on page 95)

(pictured on page 95)

## ——— Serves 8 ———

Apricot-Glazed Ham (3 ounces per serving)
Sweet Potato Crunch
Green Beans with Mushrooms and Garlic
Red-and-Green Apple Salad
Spumoni and Berries

*Total Calories per Serving: 599*
*(Calories from Fat: 19%)*

## Apricot-Glazed Ham

1  (8½-pound) smoked, reduced-sodium, fully
    cooked ham half
**About 40 whole cloves**
**Vegetable cooking spray**
**1  (10-ounce) jar no-sugar-added apricot spread**
**¾  cup unsweetened orange juice**
**1  tablespoon Dijon mustard**
**1½  teaspoons grated fresh gingerroot**
**¾  teaspoon hot sauce**

**Remove** skin from ham; trim fat. Make shallow cuts in a diamond pattern on outside of ham; insert cloves. Place ham on a rack coated with cooking spray; place in a shallow roasting pan.

**Bake** at 325° for 1 hour. Combine apricot spread and next 4 ingredients. Reserve 1 cup mixture, and set aside. Brush ham with apricot mixture; cover with aluminum foil. Bake at 325° for 2 hours or until a meat thermometer registers 140°, brushing with apricot mixture every 30 minutes.

**Warm** 1 cup reserved apricot mixture; serve with ham. **Yield: 33 (3-ounce) servings.**

PER SERVING: 122 CALORIES (32% FROM FAT)
FAT 4.3G (SATURATED FAT 1.4G)
PROTEIN 15.5G CARBOHYDRATE 5.9G
CHOLESTEROL 42MG SODIUM 682MG

## Sweet Potato Crunch

**5  cups peeled, cubed sweet potato**
    **(2 pounds)**
**1  cup unsweetened applesauce**
**1  teaspoon vanilla extract**
**½  teaspoon ground cinnamon**
**¼  teaspoon salt**
**2  egg whites**
**Vegetable cooking spray**
**½  cup firmly packed brown sugar**
**2  tablespoons all-purpose flour**
**1  tablespoon margarine, melted**

**Cook** sweet potato in boiling water to cover 15 minutes or until tender; drain and cool.

**Position** knife blade in food processor bowl; add sweet potato, applesauce, and next 3 ingredients. Process until smooth. Transfer to a large bowl; set aside.

**Beat** egg whites at high speed of an electric mixer until stiff peaks form. Gently stir one-third of egg whites into sweet potato mixture; fold in remaining egg whites. Spoon into a 1½-quart soufflé dish coated with cooking spray.

**Combine** brown sugar, flour, and margarine; sprinkle over potato mixture. Bake at 350° for 35 minutes or until set. **Yield: 8 (½-cup) servings.**

PER SERVING: 161 CALORIES (10% FROM FAT)
FAT 1.8G (SATURATED FAT 0.3G)
PROTEIN 2.5G CARBOHYDRATE 34.2G
CHOLESTEROL 0MG SODIUM 118MG

# Green Beans with Mushrooms and Garlic

2  pounds fresh green beans
2  teaspoons margarine
Vegetable cooking spray
2  cups quartered fresh mushrooms
4  cloves garlic, minced
½  teaspoon onion powder
½  teaspoon salt
¼  teaspoon pepper

**Wash** beans; remove ends, if desired. Arrange in a steamer basket over boiling water. Cover and steam 8 to 12 minutes. Remove beans, and place in a single layer on paper towels to cool.

**Melt** margarine in a large nonstick skillet coated with cooking spray. Add mushrooms and garlic; cook 3 minutes or until tender.

**Add** beans, onion powder, salt, and pepper; toss. Cook until heated. **Yield: 8 servings.**

PER SERVING: 52 CALORIES (21% FROM FAT)
FAT 1.2G (SATURATED FAT 0.2G)
PROTEIN 2.6G CARBOHYDRATE 9.6G
CHOLESTEROL 0MG SODIUM 165MG

# Red-and-Green Apple Salad

⅓  cup unsweetened apple juice
2  tablespoons lemon juice
2  tablespoons cider vinegar
1  tablespoon vegetable oil
1  teaspoon Dijon mustard
¼  teaspoon pepper
⅛  teaspoon salt
⅛  teaspoon ground cinnamon
2  small unpeeled red apples, cored and sliced
1  small unpeeled Granny Smith apple, cored and sliced
4  cups loosely packed torn leaf lettuce
4  cups loosely packed torn romaine lettuce
2  tablespoons sliced almonds, toasted

**Combine** first 8 ingredients in a jar. Cover tightly, and shake vigorously. Pour into a large serving bowl. Add apples, tossing to coat. Cover and chill up to 4 hours.

**Combine** apples and lettuces; toss gently, and sprinkle with almonds. **Yield: 8 servings.**

PER SERVING: 68 CALORIES (37% FROM FAT)
FAT 2.8G (SATURATED FAT 0.4G)
PROTEIN 1.1G CARBOHYDRATE 10.8G
CHOLESTEROL 0MG SODIUM 58MG

# Spumoni and Berries

2¼  cups lime sherbet, slightly softened
2  tablespoons chopped almonds, toasted
2¼  cups pineapple sherbet, slightly softened
2¼  cups raspberry sherbet, slightly softened
16  large fresh strawberries

**Line** an 8½- x 4½- x 3-inch loafpan with wax paper. Combine lime sherbet and 2 tablespoons almonds; spread in bottom of prepared pan. Cover and freeze 30 minutes.

**Spread** pineapple sherbet evenly over lime sherbet mixture; cover and freeze 30 minutes. Spread raspberry sherbet evenly over pineapple sherbet; cover and freeze until firm.

**Invert** onto platter, and remove wax paper; cut into 1-inch slices. Serve each slice with 2 strawberries. **Yield: 8 servings.**

PER SERVING: 196 CALORIES (12% FROM FAT)
FAT 2.6G (SATURATED FAT 0.1G)
PROTEIN 2.2G CARBOHYDRATE 42.6G
CHOLESTEROL 0MG SODIUM 113MG

# Cinco de Mayo Celebration

**Serves 8**

Mock Margaritas
Green Chile Quesadillas
Chicken Enchiladas
Southwestern Rice
Jicama-Orange Salad

*Total Calories per Serving: 718*
*(Calories from Fat: 21%)*

## Mock Margaritas

1 (6-ounce) can frozen lemonade concentrate, thawed and undiluted
1 (6-ounce) can frozen limeade concentrate, thawed and undiluted
½ cup sifted powdered sugar
3¼ cups crushed ice
1½ cups club soda, chilled
Garnish: lime slices

**Combine** first 4 ingredients in a large plastic container; stir well. Freeze mixture. Remove from freezer 30 minutes before serving.

**Spoon** mixture into container of an electric blender; add club soda. Cover and process until smooth. Pour into glasses; garnish, if desired. **Yield: 8 (¾-cup) servings.**

PER SERVING: 107 CALORIES (1% FROM FAT)
FAT 0.1G (SATURATED FAT 0.0G)
PROTEIN 0.1G CARBOHYDRATE 28.0G
CHOLESTEROL 0MG SODIUM 10MG

## Green Chile Quesadillas

1 (4.5-ounce) can chopped green chiles
8 (6-inch) corn tortillas
Vegetable cooking spray
1 cup (4 ounces) shredded part-skim mozzarella cheese
½ cup (2 ounces) shredded reduced-fat Cheddar cheese
⅛ to ¼ teaspoon ground red pepper

**Drain** chiles on paper towels.

**Place** 4 tortillas on a baking sheet coated with cooking spray. Divide cheeses and chiles evenly among 4 tortillas; spread to within ½ inch of edge. Sprinkle evenly with red pepper, and top with remaining tortillas.

**Bake** at 375° for 5 minutes or until cheese melts. Cut each into 8 wedges. **Yield: 8 (4-wedge) servings.**

PER SERVING: 117 CALORIES (33% FROM FAT)
FAT 4.3G (SATURATED FAT 2.3G)
PROTEIN 7.1G CARBOHYDRATE 13.1G
CHOLESTEROL 13MG SODIUM 174MG

## Chicken Enchiladas

5 (4-ounce) skinned and boned chicken breast halves
Vegetable cooking spray
1½ tablespoons chopped onion
1½ tablespoons chopped cilantro
1 jalapeño pepper, seeded and chopped
3 (10-ounce) cans enchilada sauce, divided
8 (6-inch) corn tortillas
1½ cups (6 ounces) reduced-fat mild Cheddar cheese
½ cup diced tomato
⅓ cup ripe olives
4 cups shredded lettuce

Chicken Enchiladas, Southwestern Rice, and
Jicama-Orange Salad

## Southwestern Rice

**3** **(10½-ounce) cans low-sodium chicken broth**
**2** **teaspoons ground cumin**
**1½** **cups long-grain rice, uncooked**
**¼** **teaspoon salt**
**½** **cup thinly sliced green onions**

**Bring** chicken broth to a boil in a Dutch oven.
Add cumin, rice, and salt; cover, reduce heat, and
simmer 20 minutes or until rice is tender and liquid is absorbed. Add green onions; toss gently.
**Yield: 8 (½-cup) servings.**

PER SERVING: 145 CALORIES (7% FROM FAT)
FAT 1.1G (SATURATED FAT 0.3G)
PROTEIN 3.8G CARBOHYDRATE 29.5G
CHOLESTEROL 0MG SODIUM 114MG

## Jicama-Orange Salad

**4** **large oranges, peeled and sectioned**
**2** **sweet red peppers, cut into strips**
**2** **cups julienne-sliced jicama**
**¼** **cup white vinegar**
**2** **tablespoons vegetable oil**
**½** **teaspoon sugar**
**¼** **teaspoon ground white pepper**
**¼** **teaspoon chili powder**

**Combine** first 3 ingredients in a medium
bowl; cover and chill.
**Combine** vinegar and next 4 ingredients in a
jar; cover tightly, and shake vigorously. Chill
thoroughly.
**Drain** orange mixture if necessary; add dressing, and toss gently. **Yield: 8 (¾-cup) servings.**

PER SERVING: 103 CALORIES (32% FROM FAT)
FAT 3.7G (SATURATED FAT 0.7G)
PROTEIN 1.5G CARBOHYDRATE 17.5G
CHOLESTEROL 0MG SODIUM 3MG

**Combine** chicken and water to cover in a
saucepan. Cook over medium heat 15 minutes;
drain and cool. Shred chicken; set aside.
**Coat** a nonstick skillet with cooking spray;
place over medium-high heat until hot. Add
onion, cilantro, and jalapeño pepper; sauté until
tender. Add 1 can enchilada sauce and chicken.
Cook 5 minutes.
**Wrap** tortillas in aluminum foil, and bake at
350° for 1 minute. Fill each tortilla with chicken
mixture; roll up, and place seam side down in a
13- x 9- x 2-inch baking dish.
**Heat** remaining 2 cans enchilada sauce; pour
over enchiladas. Top with cheese, tomato, and
olives.
**Bake** at 350° for 10 minutes or until heated.
Serve over shredded lettuce. **Yield: 8 servings.**

PER SERVING: 246 CALORIES (29% FROM FAT)
FAT 7.9G (SATURATED FAT 3.2G)
PROTEIN 24.9G CARBOHYDRATE 18.9G
CHOLESTEROL 58MG SODIUM 604MG

# Celebrate the Fourth Outdoors

── Serves 6 ──

Mesquite-Smoked Cornish Hens
Herbed Pasta and Tomato Salad
French breadsticks (2 per serving)
Fresh pears and grapes
( ½ pear and ½ cup grapes per serving)
Chilled sparkling water

*Total Calories per Serving: 460*
*(Calories from Fat: 26%)*

## Mesquite-Smoked Cornish Hens

3 (1½-pound) Cornish hens
3 small, unpeeled cooking apples, cored and
     quartered (¾ pound)
1 cup loosely packed fresh thyme
1 cup unsweetened apple juice
¼ cup low-sodium soy sauce
2 tablespoons chopped fresh parsley
½ teaspoon pepper
¼ teaspoon salt
Mesquite chips
Vegetable cooking spray

**Remove** giblets from hens, and discard. Rinse hens with cold water; remove skin, and trim excess fat.

**Stuff** hens with apple quarters, and close cavities. Secure with wooden picks, and truss (tie legs together with string).

**Combine** thyme and next 5 ingredients in a large heavy-duty, zip-top plastic bag. Add hens, turning to coat; seal. Chill 2 to 4 hours, turning occasionally. Drain, reserving marinade.

**Soak** mesquite chips in water 30 minutes. Prepare charcoal fire in smoker; let burn 20 minutes. Place mesquite on coals. Place water pan in smoker; add reserved marinade and enough hot water to fill pan.

**Coat** grill rack with cooking spray; place rack in smoker. Place hens, breast side up, on rack. Cover with smoker lid; cook 2 hours or until meat thermometer registers 180°.

**Remove** hens from smoker, and cool; split in half lengthwise, discarding apple quarters. Serve at room temperature or chilled. **Yield: 6 servings.**

PER SERVING: 168 CALORIES (33% FROM FAT)
FAT 6.1G (SATURATED FAT 1.6G)
PROTEIN 23.4G  CARBOHYDRATE 3.7G
CHOLESTEROL 71MG  SODIUM 280MG

## Herbed Pasta and Tomato Salad

4 ounces rotini (corkscrew pasta), uncooked
2 cups small cherry tomatoes, halved
1 cup peeled, chopped cucumber
½ cup chopped celery
1½ ounces provolone cheese, cut into strips
⅓ cup white wine vinegar
¼ cup chopped fresh basil
¼ cup chopped fresh parsley
1 tablespoon water
1 tablespoon olive oil
2 teaspoons chopped fresh oregano
¼ teaspoon salt
¼ teaspoon coarsely ground pepper

**Cook** rotini according to package directions, omitting salt. Drain; rinse in cold water.

**Combine** rotini, tomatoes, and next 3 ingredients in a large bowl; set aside.

**Combine** white wine vinegar and remaining 7 ingredients. Pour over pasta; toss.

**Cover** and chill at least 8 hours; toss before serving. **Yield: 6 (1-cup) servings.**

PER SERVING: 132 CALORIES (31% FROM FAT)
FAT 4.6G (SATURATED FAT 1.6G)
PROTEIN 4.9G  CARBOHYDRATE 17.5G
CHOLESTEROL 5MG  SODIUM 177MG

Mesquite-Smoked Cornish Hens and Herbed Pasta and Tomato Salad

Clockwise from front: Black Widow Snack Cake, Buzzard's Nests, Caramel-Peanut Apples, Popcorn with Pizzazz, and Monster Mash Dip

# Kids' Halloween Party

## Buzzard's Nests

2  egg whites
⅛  teaspoon cream of tartar
½  teaspoon ground cinnamon
¾  teaspoon vanilla extract
Dash of salt
⅔  cup sugar
½  (10-ounce) package large shredded whole
    wheat cereal biscuits, crushed
1  (12-ounce) package candy-coated chocolate-
    covered peanuts

**Combine** first 5 ingredients in a small mixing bowl; beat at high speed of an electric mixer until soft peaks form.

**Add** sugar, 1 tablespoon at a time, beating until stiff peaks form and sugar dissolves; stir in crushed cereal.

**Drop** mixture by level tablespoonfuls onto lightly greased cookie sheets; make an indentation in center of each with the back of a teaspoon. Place 3 peanut candies in each indentation.

**Bake** at 275° for 30 minutes. Immediately remove to wire racks. **Yield: 3 dozen.**

PER COOKIE: 78 CALORIES (29% FROM FAT)
FAT 2.5G (SATURATED FAT 1.0G)
PROTEIN 1.6G CARBOHYDRATE 12.5G
CHOLESTEROL 0MG SODIUM 14MG

## Popcorn with Pizzazz

¾  teaspoon salt
½  teaspoon onion powder
½  teaspoon garlic powder
½  teaspoon chili powder
½  teaspoon paprika
½  teaspoon ground thyme
2½  teaspoons grated Parmesan cheese
15  cups plain popped corn
Butter-flavored cooking spray

**Combine** first 7 ingredients. Coat popcorn with cooking spray; sprinkle with about one-third of seasoning mixture, and toss. Repeat procedure twice. **Yield: 30 (½-cup) servings.**

PER SERVING: 17 CALORIES (11% FROM FAT)
FAT 0.2G (SATURATED FAT 0.1G)
PROTEIN 0.6G CARBOHYDRATE 3.2G
CHOLESTEROL 0MG SODIUM 62MG

## Monster Mash Dip

4½  cups 1% low-fat cottage cheese
⅓  cup nonfat mayonnaise
3  tablespoons white vinegar
3  tablespoons grated Parmesan cheese
3  tablespoons finely chopped onion
1  tablespoon chopped fresh or frozen chives
¼  teaspoon dried dillweed
¼  teaspoon pepper

**Position** knife blade in food processor bowl; add all ingredients. Process until smooth.

**Cover** and chill at least 1 hour. Serve with assorted fresh vegetables. **Yield: 4 cups.**

PER TABLESPOON: 15 CALORIES (12% FROM FAT)
FAT 0.2G (SATURATED FAT 0.2G)
PROTEIN 2.3G CARBOHYDRATE 0.8G
CHOLESTEROL 1MG SODIUM 91MG

# Caramel-Peanut Apples

10  medium apples
10  wooden craft sticks
1  (14-ounce) package caramels
2  tablespoons water
⅔  cup honey-roasted peanuts, finely chopped
Vegetable cooking spray

**Wash** and dry apples; insert craft sticks into stem end of each apple. Set aside.

**Unwrap** caramels. Combine caramels and water in a medium bowl; microwave at HIGH 3½ to 4½ minutes or until smooth, stirring after each minute.

**Dip** two-thirds of each apple into hot caramel sauce, turning to coat. Scrape excess sauce from bottom of apples; roll coated bottoms in peanuts. Place on wax paper coated with cooking spray.

**Store** apples in refrigerator. Let stand at room temperature 15 minutes before serving to allow caramel to soften. **Yield: 10 servings.**

**Note:** For 30 Caramel-Peanut Apples, make the recipe three times. Do not triple; three packages of caramels are difficult to work with at one time.

PER APPLE: 279 CALORIES (19% FROM FAT)
FAT 5.8G (SATURATED FAT 3.2G)
PROTEIN 3.7G CARBOHYDRATE 55.1G
CHOLESTEROL 3MG SODIUM 135MG

# Black Widow Snack Cake

1  (18.25-ounce) package reduced-fat devil's
     food cake mix
Vegetable cooking spray
4  cups sifted powdered sugar
5  to 7 tablespoons skim milk
1  cup sifted powdered sugar
¼  cup unsweetened cocoa
2  tablespoons skim milk
Garnish: plastic spider

**Prepare** cake mix according to package directions, replacing eggs with 3 egg whites. Pour batter into two 8-inch square aluminum foil pans coated with cooking spray.

**Bake** at 350° for 30 to 35 minutes or until a wooden pick inserted in center comes out clean. Cool in pans on a wire rack.

**Combine** 4 cups powdered sugar and 5 to 7 tablespoons milk in a large bowl; spread a thin layer of mixture evenly over each cake.

**Combine** 1 cup powdered sugar, cocoa, and 2 tablespoons milk; spoon into a small heavy-duty, zip-top plastic bag. Close bag securely, and snip a tiny hole in bottom corner of bag; carefully pipe concentric circles onto each cake. Pipe straight lines at intervals from the inner circle through the outside circle, forming a web design. Garnish, if desired. **Yield: 32 servings.**

PER SERVING: 141 CALORIES (11% FROM FAT)
FAT 1.7G (SATURATED FAT 0.4G)
PROTEIN 1.4G CARBOHYDRATE 31.9G
CHOLESTEROL 0MG SODIUM 134MG

# Witch's Brew

3  (12-ounce) cans frozen unsweetened apple
     juice concentrate, thawed and undiluted
9½  cups water
1  cup lime juice
½  gallon lime sherbet, softened
9½  cups club soda, chilled

**Combine** first 3 ingredients in a large bowl; cover and chill. Just before serving, spoon sherbet into a large punch bowl; slowly pour apple juice mixture and club soda over sherbet, stirring gently. **Yield: 30 (1-cup) servings.**

PER SERVING: 114 CALORIES (5% FROM FAT)
FAT 0.6G (SATURATED FAT 0.0G)
PROTEIN 0.7G CARBOHYDRATE 27.4G
CHOLESTEROL 0MG SODIUM 60MG

# Festive Thanksgiving Feast

Creamy Broccoli Soup
Honey-Glazed Turkey Breast (3 slices per serving)
Cranberry Conserve (3 tablespoons per serving)
Holiday Potatoes with Chives
Lemon-Dill Green Beans
Anadama Rolls (1 per serving)
Pumpkin Cake with Orange Sauce

*Total Calories per Serving: 658
(Calories from Fat: 13%)*

## Creamy Broccoli Soup

Vegetable cooking spray
1 cup chopped onion
6 cups fresh chopped broccoli
⅔ cup thinly sliced carrot
2 (10½-ounce) cans low-sodium chicken broth
1 cup water
¾ teaspoon salt
½ teaspoon pepper
½ teaspoon dried thyme
1¼ cups skim milk
Garnish: carrot curls

**Coat** a Dutch oven with cooking spray; place over medium heat until hot. Add onion, and cook, stirring constantly, until tender.

**Stir** in broccoli and next 6 ingredients. Bring to a boil; cover, reduce heat, and simmer 15 minutes or until vegetables are tender. Remove from heat; cool slightly.

**Place** half of broccoli mixture in container of an electric blender; cover and process until smooth, stopping once to scrape down sides. Repeat procedure with remaining mixture.

**Return** to Dutch oven; stir in milk, and cook over medium heat until thoroughly heated. Spoon into serving bowls; garnish, if desired.
**Yield: 8 (1-cup) servings.**

PER SERVING: 57 CALORIES (16% FROM FAT)
FAT 1.0G (SATURATED FAT 0.3G)
PROTEIN 4.5G CARBOHYDRATE 9.5G
CHOLESTEROL 1MG SODIUM 287MG

## Honey-Glazed Turkey Breast

1 (6-pound) bone-in turkey breast, skinned
Vegetable cooking spray
⅓ cup honey
2 tablespoons frozen orange juice
     concentrate, thawed and undiluted
½ teaspoon ground allspice

**Place** turkey on a rack coated with cooking spray; place rack in a shallow roasting pan. Combine honey, orange juice concentrate, and allspice; brush over turkey.

**Cover** with aluminum foil; bake at 325° for 1 hour. Uncover and bake 1 hour or until a meat thermometer (not touching fat or bone) registers 170°, brushing frequently with honey mixture.

**Let** stand about 20 minutes before slicing.
**Yield: 16 (3-slice) servings.**

PER SERVING: 158 CALORIES (16% FROM FAT)
FAT 2.8G (SATURATED FAT 0.9G)
PROTEIN 25.1G CARBOHYDRATE 6.7G
CHOLESTEROL 58MG SODIUM 54MG

Honey-Glazed Turkey Breast, Cranberry Conserve, Holiday Potatoes with Chives, Lemon-Dill Green Beans, and Anadama Rolls

## Cranberry Conserve

**2 seedless oranges**
**½ cup sugar**
**1 cup water**
**1 (12-ounce) package fresh cranberries**
**¼ cup finely chopped celery**
**Orange cups (optional)**

**Grate** 1 tablespoon rind from oranges; set aside. Peel and section oranges over a bowl, reserving all juice from membranes. Set reserved juice and orange sections aside.

**Combine** sugar and water in a medium saucepan; bring to a boil over medium heat. Add cranberries; cook 3 minutes, stirring occasionally.

**Add** orange sections and reserved juice; cook 10 minutes, stirring frequently. Remove from heat; stir in orange rind, and cool. Stir in celery.

**Cover** and chill. Serve in orange cups, if desired. **Yield: 3 cups.**

PER TABLESPOON: 14 CALORIES (0% FROM FAT)
FAT 0.0G (SATURATED FAT 0.0G)
PROTEIN 0.1G CARBOHYDRATE 3.6G
CHOLESTEROL 0MG SODIUM 1MG

## Holiday Potatoes with Chives

4 medium baking potatoes, peeled and cut
    into ½-inch pieces (about 2 pounds)
½ cup hot skim milk
2 tablespoons fresh chopped chives or frozen
    chopped chives, thawed
2 tablespoons reduced-calorie margarine,
    melted
2 tablespoons grated Parmesan cheese
¼ teaspoon salt
⅛ teaspoon pepper

**Cook** potato in boiling water to cover 10 minutes or until very tender; drain. Return potato to saucepan, and mash with a potato masher.

**Stir** in hot milk and remaining ingredients.
**Yield: 8 (½-cup) servings.**

PER SERVING: 92 CALORIES (23% FROM FAT)
FAT 2.3G (SATURATED FAT 0.5G)
PROTEIN 4.0G CARBOHYDRATE 14.9G
CHOLESTEROL 1MG SODIUM 143MG

## Lemon-Dill Green Beans

2 pounds fresh green beans
1 tablespoon lemon juice
2 teaspoons reduced-calorie margarine,
    melted
¼ teaspoon dried dillweed
¼ teaspoon salt
⅛ teaspoon pepper

**Wash** beans; trim ends, remove strings, and cut, if desired. Arrange in a steamer basket over boiling water; cover and steam 10 minutes.

**Combine** lemon juice and next 4 ingredients; toss with green beans. **Yield: 8 (¾-cup) servings.**

PER SERVING: 41 CALORIES (15% FROM FAT)
FAT 0.7G (SATURATED FAT 0.1G)
PROTEIN 2.1G CARBOHYDRATE 8.3G
CHOLESTEROL 0MG SODIUM 89MG

## Anadama Rolls

1 package dry yeast
3 tablespoons molasses, divided
¾ cup warm skim milk (105° to 115°)
2 cups all-purpose flour, divided
⅓ cup yellow cornmeal
2 tablespoons vegetable oil
½ teaspoon salt
Vegetable cooking spray

**Combine** yeast, 1 tablespoon molasses, and skim milk in a 1-cup liquid measuring cup; let stand 5 minutes.

**Combine** yeast mixture, remaining 2 tablespoons molasses, 1 cup flour, cornmeal, oil, and salt in a large mixing bowl; beat at low speed of an electric mixer until blended. Gradually stir in remaining 1 cup flour to make a soft dough.

**Turn** dough out onto a lightly floured surface; knead until smooth and elastic (about 4 minutes). Place dough in a large bowl coated with cooking spray, turning to grease top. Cover and let rise in a warm place (85°), free from drafts, 1 hour or until doubled in bulk.

**Punch** dough down, and let rest 5 minutes. Turn dough out onto a lightly floured surface. Divide dough in half; roll each portion into a 12-inch circle on a lightly floured surface.

**Cut** each round into 12 wedges; roll each wedge tightly, beginning at wide end. Pinch to seal points, and place rolls, point side down, on a baking sheet coated with cooking spray.

**Cover** and let rise in a warm place, free from drafts, 1 hour or until doubled in bulk. Bake at 375° for 8 minutes or until browned. **Yield: 2 dozen.**

PER ROLL: 65 CALORIES (18% FROM FAT)
FAT 1.3G (SATURATED FAT 0.2G)
PROTEIN 1.6G CARBOHYDRATE 11.6G
CHOLESTEROL 0MG SODIUM 54MG

# Pumpkin Cake with Orange Sauce

Vegetable cooking spray
2 large eggs
⅔ cup sugar
¾ cup cooked, mashed pumpkin
1 teaspoon vanilla extract
¾ cup all-purpose flour
1 teaspoon baking powder
1 teaspoon ground cinnamon
½ teaspoon ground ginger
¼ teaspoon salt
¼ teaspoon ground nutmeg
⅛ teaspoon pepper
1 tablespoon powdered sugar
Orange Sauce
Garnish: orange rind strips

**Coat** a 9-inch round cakepan with cooking spray; line bottom with wax paper. Coat wax paper with cooking spray; set aside.

**Beat** eggs at high speed of an electric mixer until foamy. Add sugar, 1 tablespoon at a time, beating 2 minutes or until thick and pale. Stir in pumpkin and vanilla.

**Combine** flour and next 6 ingredients; add to pumpkin mixture, mixing well.

**Pour** batter into prepared pan; bake at 375° for 20 minutes or until a wooden pick inserted in center comes out clean. Cool in pan on a wire rack 5 minutes; remove from pan, and cool.

**Sift** powdered sugar through a wire-mesh strainer onto cake. Serve with Orange Sauce. Garnish, if desired. **Yield: 8 servings.**

## Orange Sauce

⅓ cup firmly packed light brown sugar
2 tablespoons cornstarch
1½ cups orange juice
3 tablespoons Triple Sec or other orange-
   flavored liqueur
1 teaspoon lemon juice

**Combine** all ingredients in a heavy saucepan. Bring to a boil over medium heat, stirring constantly; cook 1 minute, stirring constantly. Serve warm or cool. **Yield: 1¾ cups.**

PER SERVING: 203 CALORIES (7% FROM FAT)
FAT 1.6G (SATURATED FAT 0.5G)
PROTEIN 3.4G  CARBOHYDRATE 44.3G
CHOLESTEROL 55MG  SODIUM 94MG

Pumpkin Cake with Orange Sauce

# Holiday Open House

───── **Serves 16** ─────

Tomato-Clam Cocktail
Marinated Artichokes (2 per serving)
Pesto-Cheese Pasta Bites (3 per serving)
Shrimp Mousse (2 tablespoons per serving)
Plain crackers and melba rounds
(2 crackers and 2 melba rounds per serving)
Fruit Kabobs with Coconut Dressing (1 per serving)

*Total Calories per Serving: 210
(Calories from Fat: 15%)*

**Drain** artichokes, reserving liquid; quarter artichokes. Set aside.

**Combine** reserved liquid, lemon juice, and next 4 ingredients. Add artichokes; cover and chill 8 hours, stirring occasionally.

**Drain** artichokes, and if desired, place on a bed of radicchio leaves. **Yield: 40 appetizers.**

PER APPETIZER: 11 CALORIES (0% FROM FAT)
FAT 0.0G (SATURATED FAT 0.0G)
PROTEIN 0.7G CARBOHYDRATE 2.4G
CHOLESTEROL 0MG SODIUM 63MG

## Tomato-Clam Cocktail

2 (46-ounce) cans no-salt-added tomato juice
4 (8-ounce) bottles clam juice
½ teaspoon ground celery seeds
½ teaspoon freshly ground pepper
½ teaspoon dry mustard
¼ teaspoon garlic powder
¼ cup plus 2 tablespoons lemon juice
**Garnish: green onion fans**

**Combine** first 7 ingredients; cover and chill. Garnish, if desired. **Yield: 16 (1-cup) servings.**

PER SERVING: 36 CALORIES (3% FROM FAT)
FAT 0.1G (SATURATED FAT 0.0G)
PROTEIN 1.9G CARBOHYDRATE 8.8G
CHOLESTEROL 0MG SODIUM 140MG

## Marinated Artichokes

2 (14-ounce) cans artichoke bottoms
3 tablespoons lemon juice
1 teaspoon sugar
¼ teaspoon dried oregano, crushed
¼ teaspoon dried tarragon, crushed
**Dash of garlic powder**
**Radicchio leaves (optional)**

## Pesto-Cheese Pasta Bites

48 medium-size shell macaroni, uncooked
½ cup firmly packed fresh spinach
½ cup firmly packed fresh basil
2 tablespoons grated Parmesan cheese
¼ teaspoon ground white pepper
1 clove garlic, minced
⅓ cup light process cream cheese
1 (2-ounce) jar diced pimiento, drained

**Cook** pasta according to package directions, omitting salt; cool.

**Position** knife blade in food processor bowl. Add spinach and next 4 ingredients. Cover and process 1 minute or until smooth. Set aside.

**Place** a small amount of cream cheese in each macaroni shell. Top with spinach mixture and pimiento. **Yield: 4 dozen appetizers.**

PER APPETIZER: 10 CALORIES (36% FROM FAT)
FAT 0.4G (SATURATED FAT 0.2G)
PROTEIN 0.4G CARBOHYDRATE 1.1G
CHOLESTEROL 1MG SODIUM 13MG

Clockwise from front: Marinated Artichokes, Pesto-Cheese Pasta Bites, Tomato-Clam Cocktail, and Shrimp Mousse

## Shrimp Mousse

6 cups water
2 pounds unpeeled medium-size fresh shrimp
2 envelopes unflavored gelatin
¼ cup water
1 (8-ounce) carton plain low-fat yogurt
1 cup 1% low-fat cottage cheese
¼ cup diced green pepper
¼ cup grated onion
3 tablespoons lemon juice
2 tablespoons minced fresh parsley
1 tablespoon white wine Worcestershire sauce
2 teaspoons prepared horseradish
1 teaspoon hot sauce
¾ teaspoon salt
¾ teaspoon paprika
Vegetable cooking spray
Garnishes: parsley, carrot curls

**Bring** 6 cups water to a boil; add shrimp, and cook 3 to 5 minutes. Drain well; rinse in cold water. Cover and chill.

**Peel** shrimp, and devein, if desired. Chop shrimp; set aside.

**Combine** gelatin and ¼ cup water in a saucepan; let stand 1 minute. Cook over low heat until gelatin dissolves, stirring constantly. Remove from heat.

**Position** knife blade in food processor bowl. Combine gelatin mixture, yogurt, and next 10 ingredients in processor bowl. Process 1 minute or until smooth. Add shrimp, and stir well.

**Pour** shrimp mixture into a 5-cup mold coated with cooking spray. Cover and chill 8 hours or until firm.

**Unmold** mousse onto plate. Garnish, if desired. Serve with crackers. **Yield: 4½ cups.**

PER TABLESPOON: 16 CALORIES (17% FROM FAT)
FAT 0.3G (SATURATED FAT 0.1G)
PROTEIN 2.7G CARBOHYDRATE 0.6G
CHOLESTEROL 15MG SODIUM 56MG

## Finishing Touches

•**Green onion fans:** Cut off the white portion of onion. Slice the green portion into thin strips from one or both ends, cutting almost to, but not through, the center. Chill in ice water until strips curl.
•**Carrot curls:** Cut carrots into thin strips with a sharp vegetable peeler. Roll strips up tightly, and secure with wooden picks. Chill in ice water until set; remove picks before garnishing.

## Fruit Kabobs with Coconut Dressing

1 medium-size red apple, unpeeled
1 medium pear, unpeeled
1 tablespoon lemon juice
21 unsweetened pineapple chunks
21 seedless red or green grapes
21 fresh strawberries, capped
Coconut Dressing

**Cut** apple and pear each into 21 bite-size pieces. Add lemon juice; toss ingredients.

**Alternate** fruit on 21 wooden skewers. Serve with Coconut Dressing. **Yield: 21 appetizer servings.**

### Coconut Dressing
1½ cups vanilla low-fat yogurt
1½ tablespoons flaked coconut
1½ tablespoons reduced-calorie orange
    marmalade

**Combine** all ingredients in a bowl; stir well. Serve with kabobs. **Yield: 1⅔ cups.**

PER SERVING: 42 CALORIES (11% FROM FAT)
FAT 0.5G (SATURATED FAT 0.3G)
PROTEIN 1.0G CARBOHYDRATE 9.0G
CHOLESTEROL 1MG SODIUM 12MG

# Traditional Christmas Dinner

(pictured on page 2)

(pictured on page 2)

## ——— Serves 10 ———

Cream of Crabmeat Soup
Roast Turkey Breast and Gravy (3 ounces per serving)
Savory Cornbread Dressing
Seasoned Green Beans
Glazed Carrots
Light-Style Cranberry Relish
(2 tablespoons per serving)
Layered Ambrosia

*Total Calories per Serving: 658
(Calories from Fat: 18%)*

## Cream of Crabmeat Soup

¼ **cup diced onion**
2 **tablespoons reduced-calorie margarine,**
   **melted**
⅛ **teaspoon ground white pepper**
½ **teaspoon Beau Monde seasoning**
**Dash of mace**
½ **teaspoon hot sauce**
1 **(12-ounce) can evaporated skimmed milk**
2 **tablespoons cornstarch**
2 **cups skim milk**
½ **pound fresh crabmeat, flaked**
¼ **cup dry sherry**

**Sauté** onion in margarine in a saucepan until tender. Stir in pepper and next 4 ingredients; cook, stirring constantly, until mixture begins to boil. Combine cornstarch and 2 cups skim milk; add to hot mixture. Bring to a boil over medium heat; stir constantly. Cook 1 minute. Stir in crabmeat and sherry. **Yield: 10 (½-cup) servings.**

PER SERVING: 94 CALORIES (19% FROM FAT)
FAT 2.0G (SATURATED FAT 0.4G)
PROTEIN 8.9G CARBOHYDRATE 8.3G
CHOLESTEROL 25MG SODIUM 211MG

## Roast Turkey Breast and Gravy

1 **(5- to 5½-pound) turkey breast, skinned**
1 **medium onion**
2 **stalks celery, halved**
**Vegetable cooking spray**
1½ **tablespoons salt-free lemon-pepper**
   **seasoning**
1½ **teaspoons garlic powder**
1½ **teaspoons onion powder**
1 **teaspoon poultry seasoning**
½ **teaspoon paprika**
**Garnish: parsley sprigs**
**Gravy**

**Rinse** turkey breast; pat dry. Place onion and celery in breast cavity; spray breast with cooking spray.

**Combine** lemon-pepper seasoning and next 4 ingredients; sprinkle over breast. Place breast in a browning bag prepared according to package directions; place in a shallow pan.

**Bake** at 325° for 1 hour. Cut a slit in top of bag; bake 1 additional hour or until meat thermometer registers 170°.

**Transfer** to a serving platter. Let stand 15 minutes; carve into thin slices.

**Reserve** onion and pan drippings to make Gravy. Garnish, if desired. Serve with Gravy.
**Yield: 13 (3-ounce) servings.**

### Gravy

3 **tablespoons instant nonfat dry milk**
1 **tablespoon all-purpose flour**
½ **teaspoon chicken-flavored bouillon**
   **granules**
½ **cup water**
½ **teaspoon browning-and-seasoning sauce**

**Pour** reserved pan drippings through a gravy skimmer; reserve 1 cup broth, and discard fat. Place broth in container of an electric blender with reserved onion; cover and process until smooth.

**Pour** into a small saucepan; add nonfat dry milk and remaining ingredients. Bring to a boil; reduce heat, and simmer 5 minutes, stirring frequently. **Yield: 2 cups.**

PER SERVING: 205 CALORIES (18% FROM FAT)
FAT 4.2G (SATURATED FAT 1.3G)
PROTEIN 34.9G CARBOHYDRATE 4.7G
CHOLESTEROL 78MG SODIUM 358MG

# Savory Cornbread Dressing

1  cup yellow cornmeal
½  teaspoon baking powder
½  teaspoon baking soda
¼  teaspoon salt
¼  cup frozen egg substitute, thawed
1  cup nonfat buttermilk
1  tablespoon reduced-calorie margarine
Butter-flavored vegetable cooking spray
5  slices whole wheat sandwich bread
6  ounces ground turkey sausage
1½  cups chopped onion
1  cup chopped celery
⅓  cup frozen egg substitute, thawed
2  (10½-ounce) cans low-sodium chicken broth
1  cup evaporated skimmed milk
½  teaspoon poultry seasoning
¼  teaspoon freshly ground black pepper
⅛  teaspoon red pepper
2  tablespoons minced fresh parsley
¼  teaspoon paprika

**Combine** first 4 ingredients in a medium bowl; make a well in center of mixture.

**Combine** ¼ cup egg substitute, buttermilk, and margarine; add to dry ingredients, stirring just until moistened. Spoon into muffin pans coated with cooking spray, filling two-thirds full.

**Bake** at 450° for 10 to 12 minutes or until lightly browned; cool. Crumble muffins and bread slices into a large bowl.

**Cook** sausage, onion, and celery in a nonstick skillet coated with cooking spray, stirring until sausage is browned and crumbled. Drain and pat dry with paper towels.

**Combine** ⅓ cup egg substitute, broth, and evaporated milk; add to breadcrumbs, and let stand until liquid is absorbed. Add sausage mixture, poultry seasoning, and next 3 ingredients; stir well.

**Spoon** dressing into a 12- x 8- x 2-inch baking dish coated with cooking spray. Spray top of unbaked dressing with cooking spray; sprinkle with paprika.

**Bake** at 350° for 1 hour. **Yield: 10 (⅔-cup) servings.**

PER SERVING: 171 CALORIES (20% FROM FAT)
FAT 3.8G (SATURATED FAT 1.0G)
PROTEIN 10.6G CARBOHYDRATE 24.6G
CHOLESTEROL 13MG SODIUM 399MG

### Defat Chicken or Beef Broth

To defat commercial chicken or beef broth, place the unopened can in the refrigerator at least 1 hour before using. Open the can, and skim off the layer of solidified fat.

## Seasoned Green Beans

2  pounds fresh green beans
¼  cup chopped lean cooked ham
1  beef-flavored bouillon cube
¼  teaspoon freshly ground pepper
1½  cups water

**Wash** beans, and remove strings; cut beans into 1½-inch pieces. Place in a 5-quart Dutch oven; add ham and remaining ingredients.

**Bring** to a boil; cover, reduce heat, and simmer 20 minutes, stirring occasionally. **Yield: 10 (½-cup) servings.**

PER SERVING: 36 CALORIES (13% FROM FAT)
FAT 0.5G (SATURATED FAT 0.2G)
PROTEIN 2.7G CARBOHYDRATE 6.5G
CHOLESTEROL 3MG SODIUM 48MG

## Glazed Carrots

5  cups thinly sliced carrot
2  tablespoons brown sugar
1  teaspoon dry mustard
¼  teaspoon salt
¼  teaspoon hot sauce
1½  tablespoons reduced-calorie margarine

**Cook** carrot in a small amount of boiling water 5 to 8 minutes or until crisp-tender; drain.

**Combine** brown sugar and next 4 ingredients in a small saucepan; cook over medium heat, stirring constantly, until margarine melts. Add to carrot; toss gently. **Yield: 10 (½-cup) servings.**

PER SERVING: 40 CALORIES (29% FROM FAT)
FAT 1.3G (SATURATED FAT 0.2G)
PROTEIN 0.6G CARBOHYDRATE 7.4G
CHOLESTEROL 0MG SODIUM 96MG

## Light-Style Cranberry Relish

1  orange, unpeeled
2  cups fresh cranberries
1  cup diced unpeeled apple
1  (8-ounce) can unsweetened crushed
    pineapple, drained
⅓  cup sugar

**Position** knife blade in food processor bowl. Quarter orange; remove seeds, and place orange in processor bowl. Pulse until coarsely ground. Spoon into a medium bowl; set aside.

**Place** cranberries in processor bowl; pulse until coarsely ground. Add cranberries, apple, and remaining ingredients to orange; mix well. Cover and chill 8 hours. **Yield: 3 cups.**

PER TABLESPOON: 12 CALORIES (0% FROM FAT)
FAT 0.0G (SATURATED FAT 0.0G)
PROTEIN 0.1G CARBOHYDRATE 3.0G
CHOLESTEROL 0MG SODIUM 0MG

## Layered Ambrosia

3  cups orange sections
1  cup pink grapefruit sections
½  cup flaked coconut, divided
1  (8-ounce) can unsweetened crushed
    pineapple, undrained
3  tablespoons honey

**Arrange** half of orange sections in a glass bowl; top with grapefruit sections, ¼ cup coconut, pineapple, and remaining orange sections.

**Drizzle** with honey, and sprinkle with remaining ¼ cup coconut.

**Cover** and chill 8 hours. **Yield: 10 (½-cup) servings.**

PER SERVING: 88 CALORIES (17% FROM FAT)
FAT 1.7G (SATURATED FAT 1.5G)
PROTEIN 0.9G CARBOHYDRATE 19.0G
CHOLESTEROL 0MG SODIUM 13MG

# Festive Finales

If you thought eating healthy meant skipping dessert, here's
a little secret. You can indulge in these luscious finales—
all created with a lighter touch.

Spice Cake, Lemon Poppy Seed Cake, Chocolate-Mint Cake Roll

Frozen Chocolate Brownie Pie, Fresh Orange Sorbet, All Seasons Lemon Trifle

Chocolate-Almond Pound Cake, Chocolate-Amaretto Cheesecake, Grapefruit Ice

Apple-Cheese Bake, Apricot-Yogurt Tortoni, Blueberry Streusel Cake

Vanilla Poached Pears (recipe on page 134)

# Chocolate-Almond Pound Cake

¼ cup margarine, softened
3 tablespoons shortening
1⅓ cups sugar
3 egg whites
2¼ cups sifted cake flour
½ teaspoon baking soda
⅛ teaspoon salt
1 cup nonfat buttermilk
¾ teaspoon almond extract
1 (1-ounce) square semisweet chocolate, melted
Vegetable cooking spray

**Beat** margarine and shortening at medium speed of an electric mixer about 2 minutes or until creamy; gradually add sugar, beating at medium speed 5 to 7 minutes. Add egg whites, one at a time, beating just until blended.

**Combine** flour, soda, and salt; add to margarine mixture alternately with buttermilk, beginning and ending with flour mixture. Mix at low speed just until blended after each addition.

**Remove** 2 cups batter, and stir in almond extract. Stir melted chocolate into remaining batter.

**Alternately** spoon batters into a 9- x 5- x 3-inch loafpan coated with cooking spray. Gently swirl batter with a knife to create a marbled effect.

**Bake** at 325° for 55 to 60 minutes or until a wooden pick inserted in center comes out clean. Cool in pan on a wire rack 10 minutes; remove from pan, and cool completely on a wire rack. **Yield: 16 servings.**

PER SERVING: 181 CALORIES (28% FROM FAT)
FAT 5.6G (SATURATED FAT 1.4G)
PROTEIN 2.6G CARBOHYDRATE 30.5G
CHOLESTEROL 1MG SODIUM 118MG

# Lemon Poppy Seed Cake

1 (18.25-ounce) package reduced-fat yellow cake mix
½ cup sugar
⅓ cup vegetable oil
¼ cup water
1 (8-ounce) carton plain nonfat yogurt
1 cup frozen egg substitute, thawed
3 tablespoons lemon juice
1 tablespoon poppy seeds
Vegetable cooking spray
Lemon Glaze

**Combine** cake mix and sugar in a large mixing bowl; add oil and next 4 ingredients. Beat at medium speed of an electric mixer 6 minutes. Stir in poppy seeds.

**Pour** batter into a 10-cup Bundt pan coated with cooking spray.

**Bake** at 350° for 40 minutes or until a wooden pick inserted in center of cake comes out clean. Cool in pan on a wire rack 10 minutes. Remove from pan; drizzle with Lemon Glaze, and cool completely on wire rack. **Yield: 24 servings.**

## Lemon Glaze
½ cup sifted powdered sugar
2 tablespoons lemon juice

**Combine** powdered sugar and lemon juice, stirring until smooth. **Yield: ¼ cup.**

PER SERVING: 150 CALORIES (25% FROM FAT)
FAT 4.2G (SATURATED FAT 0.5G)
PROTEIN 3.1G CARBOHYDRATE 25.3G
CHOLESTEROL 0MG SODIUM 227MG

Lemon Poppy Seed Cake

# Spice Cake

Vegetable cooking spray
1¾ cups sugar
¼ cup vegetable oil
½ cup frozen egg substitute, thawed
3 cups all-purpose flour
1 teaspoon baking soda
¾ teaspoon baking powder
1 teaspoon ground allspice
1 teaspoon ground cinnamon
½ cup plain nonfat yogurt
¾ cup unsweetened applesauce
3 cups unpeeled, cored, finely chopped
    Granny Smith apple
1 cup chopped walnuts
1 teaspoon vanilla extract
½ teaspoon rum flavoring
½ teaspoon black walnut flavoring
½ teaspoon butter flavoring

**Coat** a 10-inch Bundt pan with cooking spray; dust with flour, and set aside.

**Beat** sugar and oil at medium speed of an electric mixer 1 minute. Add egg substitute, ¼ cup at a time, beating after each addition.

**Combine** flour and next 4 ingredients; add to sugar mixture alternately with yogurt and apple-sauce, beginning and ending with flour mixture. Mix after each addition.

**Stir** in apple and remaining ingredients. Pour batter into prepared pan.

**Bake** at 350° for 55 to 60 minutes or until a wooden pick inserted in center of cake comes out clean. Cool in pan on a wire rack 10 minutes; remove from pan, and cool on wire rack. **Yield: 24 servings.**

PER SERVING: 184 CALORIES (27% FROM FAT)
FAT 5.5G (SATURATED FAT 0.6G)
PROTEIN 3.7G CARBOHYDRATE 30.7G
CHOLESTEROL 0MG SODIUM 64MG

# Baked Alaska

1 pint chocolate sorbet, slightly softened
1 pint strawberry sorbet, slightly softened
1 (16-ounce) package angel food cake mix
⅓ cup sugar
3 tablespoons water
4 egg whites
½ teaspoon cream of tartar

**Line** a 1½-quart bowl with heavy-duty plastic wrap; spread chocolate sorbet in a 1-inch layer on bottom and sides of bowl to within 2 inches of rim. Cover with additional plastic wrap, and freeze until firm.

**Remove** additional plastic wrap, and fill chocolate shell with strawberry sorbet, smoothing it level with chocolate sorbet. Cover with plastic wrap, and freeze at least 6 hours or until very firm.

**Prepare** angel food cake mix according to package directions, baking in 2 ungreased 9-inch round cakepans. Reserve 1 layer for another use. Freeze extra layer up to 3 months.

**Place** cake on an ovenproof serving plate. Remove plastic wrap, and loosen sorbet from bowl with a rubber spatula. Invert onto cake. Remove remaining plastic wrap; return to freezer.

**Bring** sugar and water to a boil in a small saucepan. Boil, without stirring, until candy ther-mometer reaches 238°. Set aside.

**Beat** egg whites and cream of tartar at high speed of an electric mixer until stiff peaks form. Beating at high speed, pour hot sugar mixture in a slow, steady stream over egg whites. Beat until blended.

**Spread** meringue over sorbet and cake, seal-ing edges to serving plate.

**Bake** at 500° for 2 to 3 minutes or until lightly browned. Serve immediately. **Yield: 12 servings.**

PER SERVING: 216 CALORIES (1% FROM FAT)
FAT 0.3G (SATURATED FAT 0.0G)
PROTEIN 4.8G CARBOHYDRATE 49.8G
CHOLESTEROL 0MG SODIUM 297MG

Baked Alaska

Chocolate Cream Log

# Chocolate Cream Log

Vegetable cooking spray
⅔ cup sifted cake flour
1 teaspoon baking powder
3 tablespoons unsweetened cocoa
3 large eggs
1 egg white
½ cup sugar
2¼ cups vanilla low-fat ice cream, slightly softened
¾ cup chocolate syrup
¾ cup reduced-fat frozen whipped topping, thawed

**Coat** a 15- x 10- x 1-inch jellyroll pan with cooking spray; line with wax paper, and coat with cooking spray. Set aside.

**Combine** flour, baking powder, and cocoa; set flour mixture aside.

**Combine** eggs, egg white, and sugar; beat at high speed of an electric mixer 8 minutes. Fold in flour mixture. Spread batter evenly into prepared pan.

**Bake** at 400° for 8 minutes or until a wooden pick inserted in center comes out clean.

**Loosen** cake immediately from sides of pan, and turn out onto a towel. Peel off wax paper. Starting at narrow end, roll up cake and towel together; cool cake completely on a wire rack, seam side down.

**Unroll** cake. Spread with ice cream; reroll cake. Cover and freeze up to 1 month. Cut roll into 10 slices; spoon chocolate syrup evenly onto dessert plates. Top each with a cake slice and a dollop of whipped topping. **Yield: 10 servings**.

PER SERVING: 206 CALORIES (18% FROM FAT)
FAT 4.1G (SATURATED FAT 1.3G)
PROTEIN 5.1G CARBOHYDRATE 37.3G
CHOLESTEROL 71MG SODIUM 67MG

# Chocolate-Mint Cake Roll

1 (8-ounce) carton plain low-fat yogurt
Vegetable cooking spray
2 large eggs
1 egg white
¾ cup sugar
¼ cup water
1 cup sifted cake flour
3 tablespoons cocoa
1 teaspoon baking powder
⅛ teaspoon salt
1 to 2 tablespoons powdered sugar
½ cup sour cream
1 tablespoon mint-flavored liqueur
1 (12-ounce) container reduced-fat frozen
   whipped topping, thawed

**Spread** yogurt on several layers of paper towels; let stand 1 hour.

**Line** a 15- x 10- x 1-inch jellyroll pan with wax paper. Coat with cooking spray; set aside.

**Beat** eggs and egg white at high speed of an electric mixer 3 minutes or until pale. Add sugar, 1 tablespoon at a time, beating well after each addition. Add water, beating until blended.

**Combine** flour and next 3 ingredients; add to egg mixture, beating at low speed just until blended after each addition. Spread in prepared pan.

**Bake** at 350° for 8 to 10 minutes or until cake springs back when lightly touched in the center.

**Sift** 1 to 2 tablespoons powdered sugar in a 15- x 10-inch rectangle on a cloth towel. When cake is done, loosen from sides of pan; turn out onto towel. Peel off wax paper. Starting at narrow end, roll up cake and towel together; place, seam side down, on a wire rack. Cool.

**Combine** drained yogurt, sour cream, and liqueur; beat at medium speed until light and fluffy. Remove 1 cup whipped topping; cover and chill. Fold remaining whipped topping into yogurt mixture. Cover and chill at least 1 hour.

**Unroll** cake; spread with yogurt mixture.

**Reroll** cake without towel; place, seam side down, on a baking sheet. Cover and freeze 2 hours. Thaw cake in refrigerator; dollop with reserved whipped topping. **Yield: 10 servings.**

PER SERVING: 250 CALORIES (33% FROM FAT)
FAT 9.1G (SATURATED FAT 6.6G)
PROTEIN 5.3G CARBOHYDRATE 36.4G
CHOLESTEROL 51MG SODIUM 133MG

# Chocolate-Amaretto Cheesecake

½ cup teddy bear-shaped chocolate graham
   cookie crumbs, divided
Vegetable cooking spray
4 (8-ounce) packages nonfat cream cheese
2 cups sugar
⅔ cup unsweetened cocoa
⅔ cup all-purpose flour
3 tablespoons amaretto
2 tablespoons vanilla extract
½ cup frozen egg substitute, thawed
1 cup reduced-calorie frozen whipped
   topping, thawed
2 tablespoons sliced almonds, toasted

**Sprinkle** ¼ cup crumbs on bottom of a 9-inch springform pan coated with cooking spray. Set remaining crumbs aside.

**Position** knife blade in food processor bowl; add cream cheese and next 5 ingredients. Process until smooth. Add egg substitute, and process just until blended. Pour mixture into pan.

**Bake** at 300° for 45 to 50 minutes or until center is almost set. Sprinkle with remaining ¼ cup crumbs. Cool completely on a wire rack.

**Cover** and chill 8 hours. Top each slice with 1 tablespoon whipped topping, and sprinkle with almonds. **Yield: 16 servings.**

PER SLICE: 222 CALORIES (9% FROM FAT)
FAT 2.3G (SATURATED FAT 1.0G)
PROTEIN 10.9G CARBOHYDRATE 37.1G
CHOLESTEROL 10MG SODIUM 379MG

## Lemon Delight Cheesecake

1 cup graham cracker crumbs
3 tablespoons sugar
2 tablespoons margarine, melted
3 (8-ounce) packages nonfat cream cheese,
     softened
¾ cup sugar
2 tablespoons all-purpose flour
3 tablespoons lemon juice
¾ cup frozen egg substitute, thawed
1 (8-ounce) carton lemon nonfat yogurt
**Garnishes: lemon slices, fresh mint sprigs**

**Combine** first 3 ingredients; press into bottom
of a 9-inch springform pan.
   **Combine** cream cheese, ¾ cup sugar, and all-
purpose flour; beat at medium speed of an electric mixer until fluffy.
   **Add** lemon juice and egg substitute, beating
well. Add yogurt, beating well; pour into prepared pan. Cover loosely with foil.
   **Bake** at 350° for 1 hour or until set. Remove
from oven; immediately run a knife around sides
of cheesecake to loosen. Cool completely in pan
on a wire rack.
   **Cover** and chill at least 8 hours. Remove sides
of pan from cheesecake. Garnish, if desired.
**Yield: 9 servings.**
   **Note:** For a crisper crust, bake crust at 350°
for 6 to 8 minutes.

PER SERVING: 245 CALORIES (14% FROM FAT)
FAT 3.7G (SATURATED FAT 0.5G)
PROTEIN 15.0G CARBOHYDRATE 35.9G
CHOLESTEROL 14MG SODIUM 603MG

## Chocolate-Cinnamon Squares

1½ cups all-purpose flour
1 teaspoon baking powder
½ teaspoon baking soda
¼ teaspoon salt
1 cup sugar
⅓ cup unsweetened cocoa
1 teaspoon ground cinnamon
1 cup nonfat buttermilk
¼ cup frozen egg substitute, thawed
2 tablespoons margarine, melted
2 teaspoons vanilla extract
**Vegetable cooking spray**
¼ cup chopped walnuts

**Combine** first 7 ingredients in a large bowl.
Combine buttermilk and next 3 ingredients; add
to dry ingredients, stirring until blended.
   **Spoon** batter into an 8-inch square pan coated
with cooking spray; sprinkle with walnuts.
   **Bake** at 350° for 30 minutes or until a wooden
pick inserted in center comes out clean. Cool in
pan on a wire rack. **Yield: 12 servings.**

PER SERVING: 171 CALORIES (20% FROM FAT)
FAT 3.8G (SATURATED FAT 0.8G)
PROTEIN 3.8G CARBOHYDRATE 30.6G
CHOLESTEROL 1MG SODIUM 137MG

## Bourbon-Walnut Brownies

⅓ cup reduced-calorie margarine, softened
¾ cup sugar
½ cup frozen egg substitute, thawed
3 tablespoons bourbon
1 teaspoon vanilla extract
½ cup all-purpose flour
½ teaspoon baking powder
⅓ cup unsweetened cocoa
**Vegetable cooking spray**
3 tablespoons finely chopped walnuts

**Beat** softened margarine at medium speed of an electric mixer until creamy; gradually add sugar, beating well.

**Add** egg substitute, beating well. Stir in bourbon and vanilla.

**Combine** flour, baking powder, and cocoa; gradually add to margarine mixture, beating at low speed just until blended.

**Spoon** batter into an 8-inch square pan coated with cooking spray. Sprinkle with walnuts.

**Bake** at 350° for 20 to 25 minutes or until a wooden pick inserted in center comes out clean.

**Cool** in pan on a wire rack. Cut into 2- x 1-inch bars. **Yield: 32 brownies.**

PER SERVING: 46 CALORIES (35% FROM FAT)
FAT 1.8G (SATURATED FAT 0.3G)
PROTEIN 1.0G CARBOHYDRATE 6.9G
CHOLESTEROL 0MG SODIUM 24MG

vanilla. Pour mixture into a 9-inch springform pan lightly coated with cooking spray.

**Bake** at 350° for 15 minutes. Cool completely in pan on a wire rack.

**Spread** half of vanilla yogurt over brownie; cover and freeze 1 hour. Spread chocolate yogurt over vanilla yogurt; cover and freeze at least 1 hour.

**Top** with remaining vanilla yogurt. Cover and freeze at least 8 hours.

**Spoon** 1 tablespoon chocolate syrup on each dessert plate; top with frozen pie. Garnish, if desired. **Yield: 12 servings.**

PER SERVING: 258 CALORIES (17% FROM FAT)
FAT 4.8G (SATURATED FAT 1.0G)
PROTEIN 6.9G CARBOHYDRATE 46.2G
CHOLESTEROL 0MG SODIUM 205MG

# Frozen Chocolate Brownie Pie

¼ **cup margarine**
⅔ **cup firmly packed brown sugar**
½ **cup frozen egg substitute, thawed**
¼ **cup buttermilk**
¼ **cup all-purpose flour**
⅓ **cup cocoa**
¼ **teaspoon salt**
1 **teaspoon vanilla extract**
**Vegetable cooking spray**
½ **gallon vanilla nonfat frozen yogurt, slightly softened**
1 **quart chocolate nonfat frozen yogurt, slightly softened**
¾ **cup chocolate syrup**
**Garnishes: fresh strawberries, chocolate curls**

**Melt** margarine in a large saucepan over medium-high heat; add brown sugar, stirring with a wire whisk. Remove from heat; cool.

**Add** egg substitute and buttermilk; stir well.

**Combine** flour, cocoa, and salt; add to buttermilk mixture, stirring until blended. Stir in

Frozen Chocolate Brownie Pie

# Apricot-Yogurt Tortoni

1 (12-ounce) package reduced-fat vanilla
   wafers, crushed
½ gallon vanilla nonfat frozen yogurt,
   slightly softened and divided
1 teaspoon almond extract
Vegetable cooking spray
1 (18-ounce) jar apricot preserves
1 (17-ounce) can apricot halves in light syrup,
   undrained
1 (2.25-ounce) package sliced almonds,
   toasted

**Combine** vanilla wafer crumbs, 1¼ cups
vanilla yogurt, and almond extract; divide mixture in half.

**Coat** a 13- x 9- x 2-inch dish with cooking
spray. Spoon half of vanilla wafer mixture evenly into dish; spread remaining vanilla yogurt
over top.

**Spread** apricot preserves over yogurt; top
with remaining vanilla wafer mixture.

**Cover** and freeze at least 8 hours. Cut dessert
into squares; top evenly with apricots and a
small amount of syrup. Sprinkle with almonds.
**Yield: 15 servings.**

PER SERVING: 278 CALORIES (17% FROM FAT)
FAT 5.3G (SATURATED FAT 0.2G)
PROTEIN 6.5G CARBOHYDRATE 51.5G
CHOLESTEROL 0MG SODIUM 88MG

# Frozen Avocado Yogurt with Candied Lime Strips

2 ripe avocados, peeled and seeded
⅔ cup lime juice
½ cup sugar
1 quart vanilla nonfat frozen yogurt, slightly
   softened
Candied Lime Strips

**Position** knife blade in food processor bowl;
add first 3 ingredients. Process until smooth,
stopping occasionally to scrape down sides.

**Pour** into a bowl; add yogurt, stirring until
blended. Spoon into an 8-inch square pan.

**Cover** and freeze. Top each serving evenly
with Candied Lime Strips. **Yield: 4¾ cups.**

## Candied Lime Strips

¼ cup thinly sliced lime rind strips
¼ cup water
¼ cup sugar

**Cook** lime strips in boiling water to cover 5
minutes; drain.

**Combine** ¼ cup water and sugar in a small
saucepan; bring to a boil over medium heat. Add
lime strips; simmer 2 minutes.

**Remove** from heat; chill. **Yield: ¼ cup.**

PER ½-CUP SERVING: 208 CALORIES (29% FROM FAT)
FAT 6.6G (SATURATED FAT 1.0G)
PROTEIN 3.5G CARBOHYDRATE 36.9G
CHOLESTEROL 0MG SODIUM 40MG

Frozen Avocado Yogurt with
Candied Lime Strips

## Yogurt with Mocha Sauce

¼ cup sugar
2½ tablespoons unsweetened cocoa
2½ tablespoons light corn syrup
2½ tablespoons water
1 tablespoon plus 1 teaspoon semisweet
   chocolate morsels
½ teaspoon instant coffee granules
¼ teaspoon vanilla extract
1 quart chocolate nonfat frozen yogurt

**Combine** first 4 ingredients in a saucepan. Bring mixture to a boil over medium heat, stirring frequently.

**Add** chocolate morsels and coffee granules, stirring until melted. Remove from heat; cool.

**Stir** in vanilla. Spoon 1 tablespoon sauce over ½ cup nonfat frozen yogurt. **Yield: 8 servings.**

PER SERVING: 145 CALORIES (7% FROM FAT)
FAT 1.1G (SATURATED FAT 0.6G)
PROTEIN 4.1G CARBOHYDRATE 31.3G
CHOLESTEROL 0MG SODIUM 69MG

## Grapefruit Ice

⅔ cup sugar
2⅓ cups grapefruit juice
½ teaspoon grated grapefruit rind
2 cups champagne, chilled

**Combine** sugar and grapefruit juice in a saucepan; bring to a boil, stirring constantly. Cover, reduce heat, and simmer 5 minutes. Cool.

**Combine** grapefruit juice mixture, grapefruit rind, and champagne; pour into a 13- x 9- x 2-inch pan. Freeze until almost firm. Spoon mixture into a bowl, and beat at medium speed of an electric mixer until slushy. Return to pan.

**Cover** and freeze 8 hours. Spoon into sherbet dishes, and serve immediately. **Yield: 8 (1-cup) servings.**

PER SERVING: 137 CALORIES (1% FROM FAT)
FAT 0.1G (SATURATED FAT 0.0G)
PROTEIN 0.5G CARBOHYDRATE 23.8G
CHOLESTEROL 0MG SODIUM 3MG

## Fresh Orange Sorbet

2½ cups water
1 cup sugar
Orange rind strips from 2 oranges
2⅔ cups fresh orange juice
⅓ cup fresh lemon juice

**Combine** water and sugar in a saucepan; bring to a boil. Add orange rind strips; reduce heat, and simmer 5 minutes. Pour mixture through a wire-mesh strainer, discarding orange rind strips; cool completely.

**Stir** in orange juice and lemon juice, and pour mixture into freezer container of a 1-gallon hand-turned or electric freezer.

**Freeze** according to manufacturer's instructions. Pack freezer with additional ice and rock salt, and let stand 1 hour before serving. **Yield: 6 (1-cup) servings.**

PER SERVING: 182 CALORIES (0% FROM FAT)
FAT 0.1G (SATURATED FAT 0.0G)
PROTEIN 0.8G CARBOHYDRATE 46.4G
CHOLESTEROL 0MG SODIUM 2MG

Frozen Strawberry Cups and Pineapple-Yogurt Pops

## Pineapple-Yogurt Pops

1 (20-ounce) can crushed pineapple in juice,
　　undrained
1 (8-ounce) carton pineapple low-fat yogurt
1 (6-ounce) can unsweetened pineapple juice
1 teaspoon grated lemon rind

**Combine** all ingredients; pour mixture into
frozen pop molds or 12 (3-ounce) paper cups,
inserting wooden sticks.

**Cover** mixture, and freeze until firm. **Yield:
12 servings.**

PER SERVING: 55 CALORIES (5% FROM FAT)
FAT 0.3G (SATURATED FAT 0.1G)
PROTEIN 1.0G CARBOHYDRATE 12.9G
CHOLESTEROL 1MG SODIUM 11MG

## Frozen Strawberry Cups

1 (16-ounce) package frozen whole
　　unsweetened strawberries, thawed
1 (8-ounce) can unsweetened crushed
　　pineapple, drained
1 (8-ounce) carton strawberry low-fat yogurt
1 large banana, diced
¼ cup finely chopped pecans, toasted
2 tablespoons powdered sugar

**Place** strawberries in container of a food
processor or electric blender; process until
smooth.

**Spoon** strawberry puree into a bowl. Add
pineapple and remaining ingredients; stir well.

**Spoon** ⅓ cup strawberry mixture into each of
12 paper-lined muffin pans.

**Cover** and freeze. Remove from freezer 10
minutes before serving. **Yield: 12 servings.**

PER SERVING: 72 CALORIES (25% FROM FAT)
FAT 2.0G (SATURATED FAT 0.3G)
PROTEIN 1.3G CARBOHYDRATE 13.5G
CHOLESTEROL 1MG SODIUM 11MG

## Apple-Cheese Bake

Vegetable cooking spray
⅓ cup honey
1½ tablespoons reduced-calorie margarine,
　　melted
¼ teaspoon ground cinnamon
¼ teaspoon ground nutmeg
¼ teaspoon ground coriander
6 (8-ounce) cooking apples, unpeeled, cored,
　　and cut into 8 wedges
½ cup granola cereal
¼ cup firmly packed brown sugar
¼ cup all-purpose flour
3 tablespoons reduced-calorie margarine,
　　softened
½ cup (2 ounces) shredded reduced-fat
　　Cheddar cheese

**Coat** a 15- x 10- x 1-inch jellyroll pan with
cooking spray.

**Combine** honey and next 4 ingredients in a
large bowl. Add apple wedges; stir gently to coat.
Drain and arrange in jellyroll pan.

**Combine** cereal and next 3 ingredients, stirring with a fork until crumbly; sprinkle evenly
over apples.

**Bake** at 350° for 30 minutes or until apple is
tender. Sprinkle evenly with cheese; bake 5 additional minutes or until cheese melts. **Yield: 12
(4-wedge) servings.**

PER SERVING: 169 CALORIES (26% FROM FAT)
FAT 4.9G (SATURATED FAT 1.4G)
PROTEIN 2.4G CARBOHYDRATE 31.8G
CHOLESTEROL 3MG SODIUM 87MG

Blueberry Streusel Cake

# Blueberry Streusel Cake

¾ cup sugar, divided
¼ cup margarine, softened
1 large egg
1 teaspoon grated lemon rind
1½ cups all-purpose flour
½ teaspoon baking soda
½ cup plain nonfat yogurt
Vegetable cooking spray
1 tablespoon all-purpose flour
2 cups fresh blueberries
1 teaspoon ground cinnamon
⅛ teaspoon ground allspice
1 teaspoon powdered sugar

**Combine** ½ cup sugar and next 3 ingredients; beat at medium speed of an electric mixer 5 minutes.

**Combine** 1½ cups flour and baking soda; add to egg mixture alternately with yogurt, beginning and ending with flour mixture.

**Pour** batter into a 9½-inch round tart pan coated with cooking spray, spreading evenly over bottom and up sides of pan.

**Combine** remaining ¼ cup sugar, 1 tablespoon flour, and next 3 ingredients, tossing gently. Spoon over batter, leaving a ½-inch border.

**Bake** at 350° for 45 minutes or until lightly browned; cool 20 minutes on a wire rack. Sprinkle with powdered sugar. **Yield: 10 servings.**

PER SERVING: 202 CALORIES (25% FROM FAT)
FAT 5.5G (SATURATED FAT 1.1G)
PROTEIN 3.6G CARBOHYDRATE 35.4G
CHOLESTEROL 22MG SODIUM 134MG

# Peachy Melba Alaska

1 (7-ounce) loaf angel food cake
Vegetable cooking spray
12 peach halves packed in juice, drained
3 egg whites
¼ teaspoon cream of tartar
¼ cup sugar
1 teaspoon vanilla extract
1 tablespoon sliced almonds
Raspberry Sauce

**Cut** cake into 12 slices; cut each slice into a 2½-inch circle with a cookie cutter. Place on a baking sheet coated with cooking spray. Place a peach half, cut side down, on each cake; set aside.

**Beat** egg whites and cream of tartar at high speed of an electric mixer 1 minute. Add sugar, 1 tablespoon at a time, beating until stiff peaks form and sugar dissolves. Stir in vanilla.

**Spread** meringue over sides and top of each peach and cake, covering completely. Sprinkle almonds on top.

**Bake** at 400° for 8 minutes or until golden. Remove from oven, and cool.

**Place** 1 tablespoon Raspberry Sauce on each serving plate. Place Peachy Melba Alaska on sauce. **Yield: 12 servings.**

## Raspberry Sauce

2 cups fresh raspberries
½ cup unsweetened grape juice

**Place** raspberries and grape juice in container of an electric blender; cover and blend until smooth. Pour mixture through a wire-mesh strainer into a bowl; discard seeds.

**Cover** and chill. Stir sauce before serving. **Yield: ¾ cup.**

PER SERVING: 117 CALORIES (4% FROM FAT)
FAT 0.5G (SATURATED FAT 0.0G)
PROTEIN 2.6G CARBOHYDRATE 27.0G
CHOLESTEROL 0MG SODIUM 101MG

# Fresh Fruit Tartlets

1 cup wheat bran cereal
10 gingersnaps
½ teaspoon ground cinnamon
2 tablespoons reduced-calorie margarine, melted
Vegetable cooking spray
½ cup nonfat sour cream
1 tablespoon unsweetened frozen orange juice concentrate, thawed and undiluted
1 cup fresh strawberries, halved
1 kiwifruit, sliced
½ cup fresh blueberries
2 tablespoons apple jelly

**Position** knife blade in food processor bowl; add cereal and gingersnaps. Process until finely ground. Add cinnamon and margarine; process until blended.

**Press** about ¼ cup crumb mixture into each of 4 (4-inch) tart pans (with removable bottoms) coated with cooking spray.

**Bake** at 350° for 7 to 8 minutes; remove from oven, and cool.

**Combine** sour cream and orange juice concentrate; spread over crusts. Arrange fresh fruit evenly on top of crusts.

**Place** apple jelly in a heavy saucepan; cook over medium heat until melted. Brush over fruit. **Yield: 4 servings.**

PER SERVING: 223 CALORIES (27% FROM FAT)
FAT 6.8G (SATURATED FAT 1.4G)
PROTEIN 4.2G CARBOHYDRATE 38.1G
CHOLESTEROL 7MG SODIUM 200MG

# Vanilla Poached Pears

(pictured on page 119)

4 medium-size firm, ripe pears
1 tablespoon lemon juice
4 cups water
3 tablespoons vanilla extract
2 tablespoons honey
½ cup sugar
2 or 3 drops of hot water
Chocolate Sauce
Garnish: fresh mint sprigs

**Peel** pears, and core from bottom, cutting to, but not through, the stem end. Cut a thin slice from bottoms so pears stand upright. Rub lemon juice over pears.

**Combine** 4 cups water, vanilla, and honey in a large saucepan; bring to a boil. Add pears; cover, reduce heat, and simmer 15 to 20 minutes or until pears are tender. Remove pears, and cool. Discard remaining honey mixture.

**Caramelize** sugar about 30 minutes before serving pears. To caramelize, place sugar in a heavy 1-quart saucepan, and cook over medium heat, stirring constantly, until sugar melts and syrup is light golden. Stir in drops of water; let stand 1 minute.

**Insert** a meat fork at base of pear to hold. Drizzle caramelized sugar from a spoon, and quickly wrap threads around pears until a delicate web is formed. Repeat with remaining pears.

**Spoon** 2 tablespoons Chocolate Sauce on each serving plate; place pears on sauce. Garnish, if desired. Serve immediately. **Yield: 4 servings.**

## Chocolate Sauce

2 tablespoons sugar
2 tablespoons unsweetened cocoa
1 teaspoon cornstarch
½ cup water
½ teaspoon vanilla extract

**Combine** all ingredients in a small saucepan; bring mixture to a boil over medium heat, stirring constantly.

**Boil** mixture 1 minute, stirring constantly. Remove from heat, and cool. **Yield: ½ cup.**

PER SERVING: 242 CALORIES (3% FROM FAT)
FAT 0.9G (SATURATED FAT 0.3G)
PROTEIN 1.4G CARBOHYDRATE 58.3G
CHOLESTEROL 0MG SODIUM 2MG

Chocolate-Drizzled Pineapple with
Raspberry Sauce

# Chocolate-Drizzled Pineapple with Raspberry Sauce

2 cups frozen unsweetened raspberries, thawed
¼ cup water
1 tablespoon cornstarch
2 tablespoons honey
Chocolate Sauce
4 (1-inch-thick) fresh pineapple slices
Garnish: fresh mint sprigs

**Combine** raspberries and water in food processor or electric blender. Process until pureed. Pour mixture through a wire-mesh strainer into a bowl; discard seeds.

**Combine** raspberry puree, cornstarch, and honey in a saucepan. Bring to a boil over medium heat, stirring constantly. Boil 1 minute, stirring constantly. Cover and chill.

**Spoon** ¼ cup raspberry sauce and 1 tablespoon Chocolate Sauce on each serving plate, and set aside.

**Spoon** remaining Chocolate Sauce into a heavy-duty, zip-top plastic bag; seal bag. Snip a tiny hole in end of bag, using scissors.

**Place** pineapple slices over sauces on serving plates; drizzle remaining Chocolate Sauce over pineapple. Garnish, if desired. **Yield: 4 servings.**

## Chocolate Sauce

1 teaspoon cornstarch
½ cup water
2 tablespoons unsweetened cocoa
3 tablespoons honey
½ teaspoon vanilla extract

**Combine** cornstarch and water in a small saucepan; add cocoa, honey, and vanilla, stirring until smooth.

**Cook** over medium heat, stirring constantly, until mixture boils; boil mixture 1 minute, stirring constantly.

**Cover** and chill. **Yield: ½ cup.**

PER SERVING: 213 CALORIES (3% FROM FAT)
FAT 0.7G (SATURATED FAT 0.2G)
PROTEIN 1.4G CARBOHYDRATE 53.0
CHOLESTEROL 0MG SODIUM 14MG

# Chocolate Fondue

2 teaspoons cornstarch
1 cup water
¼ cup unsweetened cocoa
¼ cup sugar
1 teaspoon vanilla extract

**Combine** cornstarch and water in a small saucepan. Add cocoa and remaining ingredients; stir until smooth.

**Cook** over medium heat, stirring constantly, until mixture boils; boil 1 minute, stirring constantly. Serve warm as a dip with fresh fruit.
**Yield: 1 cup.**

PER TABLESPOON: 20 CALORIES (9% FROM FAT)
FAT 0.2G (SATURATED FAT 0.1G)
PROTEIN 0.4G CARBOHYDRATE 4.1G
CHOLESTEROL 0MG SODIUM 1MG

# Blueberry Topping

1½ cups unsweetened grape juice, divided
2 cups fresh blueberries, divided
1 tablespoon frozen unsweetened orange juice
    concentrate, undiluted
⅛ teaspoon ground cinnamon
⅛ teaspoon ground ginger
1 tablespoon plus 2 teaspoons cornstarch

**Combine** 1 cup grape juice, 1 cup blueberries, and next 3 ingredients in a saucepan. Bring to a boil; reduce heat, and simmer about 3 minutes or until blueberries pop.

**Combine** cornstarch and remaining ½ cup grape juice; stir into fruit mixture. Bring to a boil, and cook 1 minute, stirring constantly. Cool; stir in remaining blueberries.

**Serve** over vanilla low-fat frozen yogurt.
**Yield: 2½ cups.**

PER TABLESPOON: 12 CALORIES (0% FROM FAT)
FAT 0.0G (SATURATED FAT 0.0G)
PROTEIN 0.1G CARBOHYDRATE 3.1G
CHOLESTEROL 0MG SODIUM 1MG

## Raspberry-Peach Topping

1 (6-ounce) can frozen unsweetened apple
   juice concentrate, thawed and undiluted
1 cup water, divided
2 cups chopped fresh peach
3 tablespoons cornstarch
¼ teaspoon almond extract
1 cup fresh raspberries

**Combine** apple juice concentrate, ⅔ cup water, and peach in a saucepan; cook over medium heat 5 minutes or until peach is tender.

**Combine** cornstarch and remaining ⅓ cup water in a bowl. Stir into peach mixture; bring to a boil. Cook 1 minute, stirring constantly. Remove from heat; stir in almond extract, and cool.

**Stir** in raspberries before serving. Serve topping over vanilla frozen yogurt. **Yield: 3½ cups.**

PER SERVING: 11 CALORIES (0% FROM FAT)
FAT 0.0G (SATURATED FAT 0.0G)
PROTEIN 0.1G CARBOHYDRATE 2.6G
CHOLESTEROL 0MG SODIUM 1MG

## Fresh Fruit with Mint-Balsamic Tea

1½ cups water
¼ cup sugar
1 regular-size tea bag
½ cup loosely packed fresh mint sprigs
1 tablespoon balsamic vinegar
2 cups cubed fresh pineapple
1 cup cubed honeydew
1 cup cubed cantaloupe
1 cup orange sections
1 cup fresh blueberries

**Combine** water and sugar in a heavy saucepan; bring to a boil. Add tea bag and mint; remove from heat, and steep 5 minutes.

**Remove** tea bag; stir in balsamic vinegar, and let stand 5 minutes.

**Pour** mixture through a wire-mesh strainer into a bowl, discarding mint.

**Add** fruit, stirring gently to coat. Cover and chill at least 1 hour. **Yield: 5 (1-cup) servings.**

PER SERVING: 125 CALORIES (4% FROM FAT)
FAT 0.5G (SATURATED FAT 0.1G)
PROTEIN 1.2G CARBOHYDRATE 31.9G
CHOLESTEROL 0MG SODIUM 11MG

## Tropical Gazpacho

2 papayas, peeled, seeded, and chopped
2 mangoes, peeled, seeded, and chopped
2 kiwifruits, peeled and chopped
2 teaspoons grated lime rind
3 tablespoons lime juice
¼ to ½ teaspoon ground cardamom
1 teaspoon vanilla extract
3 (8-ounce) bottles papaya nectar
Garnish: carambola slices

**Combine** first 8 ingredients; cover and chill. Garnish, if desired. **Yield: 5 (1-cup) servings.**

PER SERVING: 189 CALORIES (4% FROM FAT)
FAT 0.8G (SATURATED FAT 0.0G)
PROTEIN 1.7G CARBOHYDRATE 47.2G
CHOLESTEROL 0MG SODIUM 11MG

### Savor Exotic Fruits

•**Carambola:** Also known as star fruit, its flavor is sweet and tart. Serve unpeeled, and cut into slices.
•**Mango:** The golden flesh, which tastes like a blend of peach and pineapple, clings to a large fat seed. Slice each side of the fruit along the seed to get two halves.
•**Papaya:** The sweet mellow flavor is a cross between a melon and a peach. The seeds have a peppery flavor.

Tropical Gazpacho

# Tiramisù

1 (3-ounce) package vanilla pudding mix
2 cups skim milk
1 cup mascarpone cheese
2¾ cups reduced-fat frozen whipped topping,
    thawed and divided
1 (10½-ounce) loaf angel food cake
1½ teaspoons instant coffee granules
½ cup hot water
¼ cup brandy
¼ cup Kahlúa or other coffee-flavored liqueur
Garnish: cocoa

**Combine** pudding mix and milk in a saucepan; bring to a boil over medium heat, stirring constantly. Remove from heat; cool.

**Add** mascarpone cheese; beat at low speed of an electric mixer until smooth. Fold in 1¾ cups whipped topping, and set aside.

**Slice** angel food cake in half horizontally. Cut each layer into 16 equal rectangles, and set aside.

**Dissolve** instant coffee granules in hot water; stir in brandy and Kahlúa. Brush coffee mixture over tops and bottoms of cake pieces.

**Line** bottom and sides of a 3-quart trifle bowl or soufflé dish with half of cake pieces; cover with half of pudding mixture.

**Repeat** procedure with remaining cake and pudding mixture, ending with pudding mixture. Cover and chill 8 hours.

**Spread** remaining 1 cup whipped topping over Tiramisù, and garnish, if desired. Chill. **Yield: 12 servings.**

**Note:** You may substitute 1 (8-ounce) package reduced-fat cream cheese, 3 tablespoons reduced-fat sour cream, and 2 tablespoons skim milk for 1 cup mascarpone cheese. This will save 5.4 fat grams and 46 calories per serving.

PER SERVING: 257 CALORIES (39% FROM FAT)
FAT 11.1G (SATURATED FAT 4.7G)
PROTEIN 4.6G CARBOHYDRATE 29.5G
CHOLESTEROL 18MG SODIUM 174MG

# Luscious Flan

¼ cup sugar
1 (12-ounce) can evaporated skimmed milk
½ cup skim milk
¾ cup frozen egg substitute, thawed
¼ cup sugar
⅛ teaspoon salt
½ teaspoon almond extract
½ cup fresh strawberries
1 cup seedless grapes
½ cup sliced kiwifruit

**Sprinkle** ¼ cup sugar in a heavy saucepan, and place over medium heat. Cook, stirring constantly, until sugar melts and syrup is light golden. Pour syrup into six 6-ounce custard cups, and cool.

**Combine** milks in a medium saucepan, and heat until bubbles form around edge of pan.

**Combine** egg substitute and next 3 ingredients; beat well. Gradually stir about 1 cup hot milk into egg mixture; add to remaining milk, stirring constantly.

**Pour** mixture evenly into custard cups; cover with aluminum foil. Place custard cups in a shallow pan, and pour hot water in pan to a depth of 1 inch.

**Bake** at 325° for 25 minutes or until a knife inserted near center comes out clean.

**Remove** custard cups from water, and chill at least 4 hours.

**Loosen** edges of custard with a spatula; invert onto serving plates. Arrange assorted fresh fruit around sides. **Yield: 6 servings.**

PER SERVING: 167 CALORIES (3% FROM FAT)
FAT 0.5G (SATURATED FAT 0.1G)
PROTEIN 8.7G CARBOHYDRATE 32.5G
CHOLESTEROL 3MG SODIUM 170MG

Luscious Flan

# All Seasons Lemon Trifle

1 (14.5-ounce) package angel food cake mix
1 (14-ounce) can low-fat sweetened condensed
   milk
2 teaspoons grated lemon rind
⅓ cup fresh lemon juice
1 (8-ounce) carton lemon nonfat yogurt
1 (8-ounce) container reduced-fat frozen
   whipped topping, thawed and divided
1 cup sliced fresh strawberries
1 cup fresh blueberries or blackberries
1 cup fresh raspberries
½ cup flaked coconut, lightly toasted

**Prepare** cake mix according to package directions; bake in a 10-inch tube pan. Invert pan, and cool completely.

**Cut** cake into bite-size pieces, and set aside.

**Combine** sweetened condensed milk and next 3 ingredients. Fold in 2 cups whipped topping, and set aside.

**Place** one-third of cake pieces in bottom of a 4-quart trifle bowl; top with one-third of lemon mixture. Top with strawberries. Repeat layers twice, using remaining cake pieces, lemon mixture, blueberries, and raspberries, ending with raspberries.

**Spread** remaining whipped topping over raspberries; sprinkle with coconut.

**Cover** and chill 8 hours. **Yield: 16 servings.**

**Note:** You may substitute 1 (16-ounce) angel food cake for cake mix. Cut cake into bite-size pieces, and proceed as directed.

PER SERVING: 238 CALORIES (16% FROM FAT)
FAT 4.1G (SATURATED FAT 2.8G)
PROTEIN 5.7G CARBOHYDRATE 45.3G
CHOLESTEROL 1MG SODIUM 244MG

# Tropical Trifle

1 (3-ounce) package vanilla pudding mix
2 cups skim milk
1 (16-ounce) package fat-free pound cake
½ cup unsweetened orange juice
1 (10-ounce) package frozen sliced
   strawberries, thawed and undrained
1 (20-ounce) can crushed unsweetened
   pineapple, undrained
2 bananas, peeled and sliced
1 (8-ounce) container reduced-fat frozen
   whipped topping, thawed
¼ cup flaked coconut, toasted

**Combine** pudding mix and skim milk in a large saucepan; bring to a boil over medium heat, stirring constantly. Remove from heat, and cool.

**Cut** pound cake into 10 slices; cut each slice into 6 cubes.

**Place** half of cake cubes in bottom of a 2½-quart trifle bowl. Sprinkle with half of orange juice.

**Spoon** half of strawberries with juice over cubes; spread with half of pudding.

**Combine** undrained pineapple and banana slices, stirring to coat. Drain fruit; discard liquid.

**Spoon** half of fruit mixture over pudding; spread half of whipped topping over top. Repeat layers, ending with whipped topping. Sprinkle with coconut.

**Cover** with plastic wrap, and chill at least 6 hours. **Yield: 12 servings.**

PER SERVING: 258 CALORIES (11% FROM FAT)
FAT 3.2G (SATURATED FAT 0.5G)
PROTEIN 4.0G CARBOHYDRATE 53.3G
CHOLESTEROL 13MG SODIUM 280MG

# Index